Ninja Foodi Grill Cookbook

100 Quick, Easy and Delicious Recipes for Indoor Grilling and Air Frying Perfection

Keven Abernathy

Copyright©2020 - All rights reserved.

Disclaimer Notice:

Please note the information contained within this document is for educational and entertainment purposes only. Every attempt has been made to provide accurate, up to date and reliable, complete information. No warranties of any kind are expressed or implied. Readers acknowledge that the author is not engaging in the rendering of legal, financial, medical or professional advice. By reading this document, the reader agrees that under no circumstances are we responsible for any losses, direct or indirect, which are incurred as a result of the use of information contained within this document, including, but not limited to, errors, omissions, or inaccuracies.

Legal Notice:

This book is copyright protected. This is only for personal use. You cannot amend, distribute, sell, use, quote or paraphrase any part or the content within this book without the consent of the author or copyright owner. Legal action will be pursued if this is breached.

The information provided herein is stated to be truthful and consistent, in that any liability, regarding inattention or otherwise, by any usage or abuse of any policies, processes, or directions contained within is the solitary and complete responsibility of the recipient reader. Under no circumstances will any legal liability or blame be held against the publisher for any reparation, damages, or monetary loss due to the information herein, either directly or indirectly. Respective authors own all copyrights not held by the publisher.

The author is not a licensed practitioner, physician or medical professional and offers no medical treatment, diagnoses, suggestions or counselling. The information presented herein has not been evaluated by the US Food & Drug Administration, and it is not intended to diagnose, treat, cure or prevent any disease. Full medical clearance from a licensed physician should be obtained before beginning or modifying any diet, exercise or lifestyle program, and physician should be informed of all nutritional changes. The author claims no responsibility to any person or entity for any liability, loss, damage or death caused or alleged to be caused directly or indirectly as a result of the use, application or interpretation of the information presented herein.

Table of Contents

1. Introduction 7

2. About Ninja Foodi Grill 9

3. Breakfast 11

   3.1 Tomato and Bacon Morning Omelet 11

   3.2 Creative Potato Pancakes 12

   3.3 Grilled Up Maple Flavored Broccoli 13

   3.4 Plate-O-Bagels 15

   3.5 Original French Pineapple Toast 16

   3.6 Cool Potato Pancakes 17

   3.7 Early Morning Bacon Egg Muffins 19

   3.8 Airy Mac and Cheese 20

   3.9 Magical Sausage and Kale 21

   3.10 Blister Green Beans 22

4. Appetizers & Snacks 25

   4.1 Honey Mustard Chicken Tenders 25

   4.2 Cajun Eggplant Appetizer 26

   4.3 Fajita Skewers 27

   4.4 Honey Asparagus 28

   4.5 Crispy Potato Cubes 29

   4.6 Healthy Onion Rings 30

   4.7 Lemon-Garlic Shrimp Caesar Salad 31

   4.8 Bacon Brussels Delight 32

   4.9 Seared Tuna Salad 33

   4.10 Portobello and Pesto Sliders 35

4.11 Crispy Rosemary Potatoes 36

4.12 Simple Crispy Brussels 37

5. Delicious Poultry 39

5.1 Alfredo Flavored Apple Chicken 39

5.2 Maple Flavored Chicken 40

5.3 Classic Chicken Tomatina 41

5.4 Chicken Chili and Beans 43

5.5 Hearty Chicken Tomatina 44

5.6 Orange Flavored Chicken Fiesta 45

5.7 Thai Baked Soy Chicken 47

5.8 Seasoned Turkey Cutlets 48

5.9 Soy Flavored Thai Chicken 49

5.10 Tomato and Turkey Meal 51

5.12 Zucchini and Chicken Kabobs 52

6. Fish & Seafood 55

6.1 Coconut Baked Trout 55

6.2 Shrimp Pie Meal 56

6.3 Juicy Rosemary Garlic Salmon 58

6.4 Mustard Crispy Cod 59

6.5 Buttery Spiced Grilled Salmon 60

6.6 Crispy Crabby Patties 62

6.7 Spicy Grilled Shrimps 63

6.8 Baked Parmesan Fish 64

6.9 Roast BBQ Shrimp 65

6.10 Wholesome Broccoli Shrimp 66

6.11 Creamed Salmon 68

6.12 Cream Mussels with Bread 69

6.13 Cod Sandwich 71

6.14 Classic Honey Salmon 73

6.15 Sausage Potato Shrimp 74

6.16 Crispy Garlic Mackerel 75

7. Pork, Beef & Lamb 77

7.1 Kale Sausage Soup 77

7.2 Spinach Beef Meatloaf 78

7.3 Steak Pineapple Mania 80

7.4 Avocado Salsa Steak 82

7.5 Bourbon Pork Chops 83

7.6 Korean Chili Pork 85

7.7 Lettuce Cheese Steak 86

7.8 Grilled Beef Burgers 88

8. Meatless Recipes 91

8.1 Rice & Bean Meal 91

8.2 Bacon Potato Soup 92

8.3 Pasta Squash Soup 94

8.4 Mustard Green Veggies 95

8.5 Creamy Corn Potatoes 97

8.6 Eggplant Pasta Delight 99

8.7 Healthy Broccoli Salad 101

8.8 Veggie Rice Soup 102

9. Vegetarian 105

9.1 Tomato Salsa 105

9.2 Mushroom Tomato Roast 106

9.3 Cheddar Cauliflower Meal 108

9.4 Buttery Spinach Meal 109

9.5 Mustard Green Veggie Meal 110

9.6 Broccoli and Arugula Salad 112

9.7 Mustard Green Veggies 114

9.8 Creamy Corn Potatoes 116

9.9 Classic Bruschetta 117

10. Dessert 121

10.1 Cashew Cream 121

10.2 Blackberry Cake 122

10.3 The Original Pot-De-Crème 123

10.4 Cinnamon Bun 124

10.5 Lemon Mousse 125

10.6 Chocolate Cheesecake 126

10.7 Vanilla Yogurt 127

10.8 Coffee Custard 129

10.9 Chocolate Fudge 130

10.10 Lime Cheesecake 131

10.11 Lemon Cheesecake 133

10.12 Strawberry Crumble 135

10.13 Peanut Butter Cups 136

10.14 Chocolate Brownies 137

10.15 Cream Crepes 138

10.16 Nut Porridge 139

11. Conclusion 141

1. Introduction

The Ninja Food Grill is an indoor electric grill! With virtually no smoke, all of your favorite dishes can be grilled, roasted, and air fried!

It's hard to make room for single-purpose countertop appliances, even in the most organized and spacious kitchens. So often, you're going to use a commodity a few times to relegate the cumbersome one-trick pony to the wardrobe, the attic, or even the tag sale. But items that can do more than one thing, and do them well, on your countertop might be worth giving a permanent home.

The newest device is crying out for space? The Ninja Foodi Grill, one of the most recent additions to a growing Foodi products ecosystem. It may also air fry, bake, roast, and dehydrate, in addition to grilling. Here's the lowdown on whether one of our favorite indoor grills is worth the big bucks it's currently selling for — or whether you'd be better off with another.

2. About Ninja Foodi Grill

Even within the most organized and spacious kitchens, it's tough to make room for unmarried-motive countertop home equipment. So frequently you'll use a product a handful of instances, most effective to relegate the cumbersome one-trick pony to the closet, the attic, or maybe the tag sale. But products which could do multiple issue, and do them nicely, perhaps worth giving a permanent domestic for your countertop.

The most modern device clamoring for space? The Ninja Foodi Grill, one of the most recent additions to a developing environment of Foodi merchandise. In addition to grilling, it is able to also air fry, bake, roast, and dehydrate. Here's the lowdown on whether it's really worth the large greenbacks it's presently selling for—or whether you'd be better off with any other one of our favorite indoor grills.

The Ninja Foodi Grill is huge and it's boxy—7 inches long with the aid of 14 inches wide with the aid of 11 inches tall. To give you an idea of just how massive that is, believe an all-in-one printer, or a completely big bread field. The grill is built of brushed stainless steel and has a black plastic domed lid.

With the grill, you get a hefty grill grate, a crisper basket, and a cooking pot which can be all lined with a ceramic nonstick end. A cleaning brush and kebab skewers also are protected.

As you may think, this Foodi can grill. Although it cooks with the lid closed, the lid doesn't press down on food, so its simplest brands grill marks on one aspect at a time in case you want a Panini, you'll have to turn it over midway thru cooking. The grate leaves curved grill marks rather than immediately lines on food.

In addition to grilling, the Ninja Food Grill can air fry, roast, bake, and dehydrate, which overlaps with a number of the functions of the Ninja Foodi Pressure Cooker and Ninja Foodi Oven.

3. Breakfast

3.1 Tomato and Bacon Morning Omelet

Prep Time: 10 minutes

Cooking Time: 10 minutes

Serving: 4

Ingredients:

- 4 whole eggs, whisked
- 1 tablespoon cheddar, grated
- ¼ pound bacon, cooked and chopped
- 4 tomatoes, cubed
- 1 tablespoon parsley, chopped
- 1 tablespoon olive oil
- Salt and pepper to taste

Directions:

1. Take a small pan and place it over medium heat, add bacon and Sauté for 2 minutes until crisp
2. Take a bowl and add bacon, add remaining ingredients, and gently stir. Sprinkle cheese on top
3. Preheat Ninja Foodi by pressing the "BAKE" option and setting it to "400 Degrees F" and timer to 10 minutes
4. Let it preheat until you hear a beep
5. Pour mixture into a baking dish and transfer baking dish inside Ninja Foodi Grill, let it bake for 8 minutes
6. Serve and enjoy!

Nutrition:

- Calories: 311
- Fat: 16 g
- Saturated Fat: 4 g
- Carbohydrates: 23 g
- Fiber: 4 g
- Sodium: 149 mg
- Protein: 22 g

3.2 Creative Potato Pancakes

Prep Time: 10 minutes
Cooking Time: 24 minutes
Serving: 4
Ingredients:

- 4 medium potatoes, peeled and cleaned
- 1 medium onion, chopped
- 1 beaten egg
- ¼ cup milk
- 2 tablespoons unsalted butter
- ½ teaspoon garlic powder
- ¼ teaspoon salt
- 3 tablespoons all-purpose flour
- Pepper as needed

Directions:

1. Peel your potatoes and shred them up
2. Soak the shredded potatoes under cold water to remove starch

3. Drain the potatoes
4. Take a bowl and add eggs, milk, butter, garlic powder, salt, and pepper
5. Add in flour
6. Mix well
7. Add the shredded potatoes
8. Preheat Ninja Foodi by pressing the "AIR CRISP" option and setting it to "390 Degrees F" and timer to 24 minutes
9. let it preheat until you hear a beep
10. Add ¼ cup of the potato pancake batter to your cooking basket and cook for 12 minutes until the golden-brown texture is seen
11. Enjoy!

Nutrition:

- Calories: 240
- Fat: 11 g
- Saturated Fat: 4 g
- Carbohydrates: 33 g
- Fiber: 2 g
- Sodium: 259 mg
- Protein: 6

3.3 Grilled Up Maple Flavored Broccoli

Prep Time: 5-10 minutes

Cooking Time: 10 minutes

Serving: 4

Ingredients:

- 2 heads broccoli, cut into florets

- 4 tablespoons soy sauce
- 2 tablespoons canola oil
- 4 tablespoons balsamic vinegar
- 2 teaspoons maple syrup
- Red pepper flakes and sesame seeds for garnish

Directions:

1. Take a mixing bowl and add soy sauce, balsamic vinegar, oil, maple syrup and whisk well
2. Add broccoli and let it sit
3. Take your Ninja Foodi Grill and press "GRILL" and set to "MAX" mode, set the timer to 10 minutes
4. Let it preheat
5. Once you hear the beat, add broccoli over the grill grate
6. Lock lid and cook until the timer reads zero
7. Serve and enjoy with a topping of pepper flakes and sesame seeds

Nutrition:

- Calories: 141
- Fat: 7 g
- Saturated Fat: 1 g
- Carbohydrates: 14 g
- Fiber: 4 g
- Sodium: 853 mg
- Protein: 4 g

3.4 Plate-O-Bagels

Prep Time: 5-10 minutes

Cooking Time: 8 minutes

Serving: 4

Ingredients:

- 1 cup fine sugar
- 2 tablespoons black coffee, prepared and cooled down
- 4 bagels, halved
- ¼ cup of coconut milk
- 2 tablespoons coconut flakes

Directions:

1. Take your Ninja Foodi Grill and open lid, arrange grill grate and close top
2. Preheat Ninja Foodi by pressing the "GRILL" option and setting it to "MEDIUM" and timer to 8 minutes
3. let it preheat until you hear a beep
4. Arrange bagels over grill grate, lock lid and cook for 2 minutes, flip sausages and cook for 2 minutes more
5. Grill remaining Bagels similarly
6. Take a mixing bowl and mix remaining ingredients, pour the sauce over grilled bagels
7. Serve and enjoy!

Nutrition:

- Calories: 300
- Fat: 23 g
- Saturated Fat: 12 g
- Carbohydrates: 42 g

- Fiber: 4 g
- Sodium: 340 mg
- Protein: 18 g

3.5 Original French Pineapple Toast

Prep Time: 5-10 minutes
Cooking Time: 15 minutes
Serving: 4
Ingredients:

- 10 bread slices
- ¼ cup of sugar
- ¼ cup milk
- 3 large whole eggs
- 1 cup of coconut milk
- 10 slices pineapple, peeled
- ½ cup coconut flakes
- Cooking spray as needed

Directions:

1. Take a mixing bowl and whisk in coconut milk, sugar, eggs, milk and stir well
2. Dup breads in the mixture and keep the mon the side for 2 minutes
3. Pre-heat Ninja Foodi by pressing the "GRILL" option and setting it to "MED" and timer to 15 minutes
4. Let it pre-heat until you hear a beep

5. Arrange bread slices over grill grate, lock lid and cook for 2 minutes. Flip and cook for 2 minutes more, let them cook until the timer reads 0
6. Repeat with remaining slices, serve and enjoy!

Nutrition:

- Calories: 202
- Fat: 15 g
- Saturated Fat: 3 g
- Carbohydrates: 49 g
- Fiber: 3 g
- Sodium: 524 mg
- Protein: 8 g

3.6 Cool Potato Pancakes

Prep Time: 10 minutes

Cooking Time: 24 minutes

Serving: 4

Ingredients:

- 4 medium potatoes, peeled and cleaned
- 1 medium onion, chopped
- 1 beaten egg
- ¼ cup milk
- 2 tablespoons unsalted butter
- ½ teaspoon garlic powder
- ¼ teaspoon salt
- 3 tablespoons all-purpose flour

- Pepper as needed

Directions:

12. Peel your potatoes and shred them up
13. Soak the shredded potatoes under cold water to remove starch
14. Drain the potatoes
15. Take a bowl and add eggs, milk, butter, garlic powder, salt, and pepper
16. Add in flour
17. Mix well
18. Add the shredded potatoes
19. Pre-heat Ninja Foodi by pressing the "AIR CRISP" option and setting it to "390 Degrees F" and timer to 24 minutes
20. let it pre-heat until you hear a beep
21. Add ¼ cup of the potato pancake batter to your cooking basket and cook for 12 minutes until the golden-brown texture is seen
22. Enjoy!

Nutrition:

- Calories: 240
- Fat: 11 g
- Saturated Fat: 4 g
- Carbohydrates: 33 g
- Fiber: 2 g
- Sodium: 259 mg
- Protein: 6 g

3.7 Early Morning Bacon Egg Muffins

Prep Time: 5 minutes

Cooking Time: 7-10 minutes

Serving: 4

Ingredients:

- 1 whole egg
- 2 streaky bacon
- 1 English muffin
- Salt and pepper to taste

Directions:

1. Pre-heat Ninja Foodi by pressing the "AIR CRISP" option and setting it to "200 Degrees F" and timer to 10 minutes
2. let it pre-heat until you hear a beep
3. Take an ovenproof bowl and crack in an egg
4. Take Ninja Foodi cooking basket and add bacon, egg, and muffin into Fryer
5. Cook for 7 mutes
6. Assemble muffin done by packing bacon and egg on top of English muffin
7. **Serve and enjoy!**

Nutrition:

- Calories: 600
- Fat: 40 g
- Saturated Fat: 10 g
- Carbohydrates: 30 g
- Fiber: 5 g

- Sodium: 526 mg
- Protein: 24 g

3.8 Airy Mac and Cheese

Prep Time: 10 minutes
Cooking Time: 10 minutes
Serving: 4
Ingredients:

- 1 cup elbow macaroni
- ½ cup broccoli
- ½ cup warmed milk
- 1 and ½ cheddar cheese, grated
- Salt and pepper to taste
- 1 tablespoon parmesan cheese, grated

Directions:

1. Pre-heat Ninja Foodi by pressing the "AIR CRISP" option and setting it to "400 Degrees F" and timer to 10 minutes
2. let it pre-heat until you hear a beep
3. Take a pot and add water, allow it to boil
4. Add macaroni and veggies and broil for about 10 minutes until the mixture is Al Dente
5. Drain the pasta and vegetables
6. Toss the pasta and veggies with cheese
7. Season with some pepper and salt and transfer the mixture to your Foodi
8. Sprinkle some more parmesan on top and cook for about 15 minutes.

9. Allow it to cool for about 10 minutes once done
10. Enjoy!

Nutrition:
- Calories: 180
- Fat: 11 g
- Saturated Fat: 3 g
- Carbohydrates: 14 g
- Fiber: 2 g
- Sodium: 147 mg
- Protein: 6 g

3.9 Magical Sausage and Kale

Prep Time: 10 minutes
Cooking Time: 10 minutes
Serving: 4
Ingredients:
- 1 medium sweet yellow onion
- 4 medium eggs
- 4 sausage links
- 2 cups kale, chopped
- 1 cup mushrooms
- Olive oil as needed

Directions:
1. Take your Ninja Foodi Grill and open lid, arrange grill grate and close top

2. Preheat Ninja Foodi by pressing the "GRILL" option and setting it to "HIGH" and timer to 5 minutes
3. let it preheat until you hear a beep
4. Arrange sausages over grill grate, lock lid and cook for 2 minutes, flip sausages and cook for 3 minutes more
5. Take sausages out
6. Take a baking pan and spread onion, kale, mushrooms, sausages and crack eggs on top
7. Arrange pan inside the grill and used the "BAKE" option to bake it at 350 degrees F for 5 minutes
8. Once done, open lid and serve
9. Enjoy!

Nutrition:

- Calories: 236
- Fat: 12 g
- Saturated Fat: 2 g
- Carbohydrates: 17 g
- Fiber: 4 g
- Sodium: 369 mg
- Protein: 18 g

3.10 Blister Green Beans

Prep Time: 5 minutes

Cooking Time: 10 minutes

Serving: 4

Ingredients:

- 1-pound green beans, trimmed

- 2 tablespoons vegetable oil
- 1 lemon, juiced
- Pinch of red pepper flakes
- Flaky sea salt as needed
- Fresh ground black pepper as needed

Directions:
1. Take a medium-sized bowl and add green beans
2. Preheat Ninja Foodi by pressing the "GRILL" option and setting it to "MAX" and timer to 10 minutes
3. Let it preheat until you hear a beep
4. Once preheated, transfer green beans to Grill Grate
5. Lock lid and let them grill for 8-10 minutes, making sure to toss them from time to time until all sides are blustered well
6. Squeeze lemon juice over green beans and top with red pepper flakes, season with salt and pepper

Nutrition:
- Calories: 100
- Fat: 7 g
- Saturated Fat: 1 g
- Carbohydrates: 10 g
- Fiber: 4 g
- Sodium: 30 mg
- Protein: 2 g

4. Appetizers & Snacks

4.1 Honey Mustard Chicken Tenders

Prep Time: 5 minutes
Cooking Time: 3 minutes
Servings: 4
Ingredients:

- 2 pounds chicken tenders
- 1/2 cup Dijon mustard
- 1/2 cup walnuts
- 2 tablespoons honey
- 2 tablespoons olive oil
- 1 teaspoon black pepper, ground

Directions:

1. Grab a bowl, using a whisk mix the mustard, olive oil, honey, and pepper into it
2. Add the chicken and toss to coat
3. Grind the walnut in your food processor
4. Supplement the flame broil mesh and close the hood
5. Pre-heat Ninja Foodi by pressing the "GRILL" option and setting it to "HIGH" for 4 minutes
6. Toss the chicken tenders in the ground walnuts to coat them lightly
7. Grill the chicken tender for 3 minutes
8. Serve hot and enjoy!

Nutrition:

- Calories: 444 kcal

- Carbs: 26 g
- Fat: 20 g.
- Protein: 6 g

4.2 Cajun Eggplant Appetizer

Prep Time: 5-10 minutes
Cooking Time: 10 minutes
Servings: 8
Ingredients:

- 2 small eggplants cut into slices
- 1/4 cup olive oil
- 2 tablespoons lime juice
- 3 teaspoons Cajun seasoning

Directions:

1. Coat the eggplant slices with oil, lemon juices and Cajun seasoning add the chicken wings and combine well to coat
2. Arrange the grill grate and close the lid
3. Pre-heat Ninja Foodi by pressing the "GRILL" option and setting it to "MED" and timer to 10 minutes
4. Let it pre-heat until you hear a beep
5. Arrange the eggplant slices over the grill grate, lock lid and cook for 5 minutes
6. Flip the chicken and close the lid, cook for 5 minutes more
7. Serve warm and enjoy!

Nutrition:

- Calories: 362 kcal

- Carbs: 16 g
- Fat: 11 g.
- Protein: 8 g

4.3 Fajita Skewers

Prep Time: 10 minutes
Cooking Time: 14 minutes
Servings: 8
Ingredients:

- 1-pound sirloin steak, cubed
- Olive oil, for drizzling
- 1 bunch scallions cut into large pieces
- 4 large bell pepper, cubed
- 1 pack tortillas, torn
- Salt to taste
- Black pepper, grounded

Directions:

- Thread the steak, tortillas, scallions, and pepper on the skewers
- Drizzle olive oil, salt, black pepper over the skewers
- Pre-heat Ninja Foodi by pressing the "GRILL" option and setting it to "MED"
- Once preheated, open the lid and place 4 skewers on the grill
- Cover the lid and grill for 7 minutes
- Keep rotating skewers for every 2 minutes
- Serve warm and enjoy!

Nutrition:

- Calories: 353 kcal
- Carbs: 11 g
- Fat: 7.5 g.
- Protein: 13.1 g

4.4 Honey Asparagus

Prep Time: 10 minutes

Cooking Time: 15 minutes

Servings: 4

Ingredients:

- 2 pounds asparagus, trimmed
- 1/2 teaspoon pepper
- 1 teaspoon salt
- 1/4 cup honey
- 2 tablespoons olive oil
- 4 tablespoons tarragon, minced

Directions:

1. Take a bowl and add asparagus, oil, salt, honey, pepper, tarragon and toss well
2. Pre-heat Ninja Foodi by pressing the "GRILL" option and setting it to "MED" and timer to 8 minutes
3. Let it pre-heat until you hear a beep
4. Arrange asparagus over grill grate, lock lid and cook for 4 minutes, flip asparagus and cook for 4 minutes more
5. Serve and enjoy!

Nutrition:

- Calories: 240 kcal
- Carbs: 31 g
- Fat: 15 g.
- Protein: 7 g

4.5 Crispy Potato Cubes

Prep Time: 10 minutes
Cooking Time: 20 minutes
Servings: 4
Ingredients:

- 1-pound potato, peeled
- 1 tablespoon olive oil
- 1 teaspoon dried dill
- 1 teaspoon dried oregano
- 1/4 teaspoon chili flakes

Directions:

1. Pre-heat Ninja Foodi by squeezing the "AIR CRISP" alternative and setting it to "400 Degrees F" and timer to 20 minutes
2. Let it pre-heat until you hear a beep
3. Cut potatoes into cubes
4. Sprinkle potato cubes with dill, oregano and chili flakes
5. Transfer to Foodi Grill and cook for 15 minutes
6. Stir while cooking, once they are crunchy
7. Serve and enjoy!

Nutrition:

- Calories: 119 kcal
- Carbs: 20 g
- Fat: 4 g.
- Protein: 12 g

4.6 Healthy Onion Rings

Prep Time: 10 minutes
Cooking Time: 10 minutes
Servings: 4
Ingredients:

- 1/4 teaspoon salt
- 1 egg
- 3/4 cup milk
- 1 tablespoon baking powder
- 3/4 cup breadcrumbs
- 1 large onion
- 1 cup flour
- 1 teaspoon paprika

Directions:

1. Pre-heat Ninja Foodi by squeezing the "AIR CRISP" alternative and setting it to "340 Degrees F" and timer to 10 minutes
2. Let it pre-heat until you hear a beep
3. Take a bowl and whisk the egg, milk, salt, flour, paprika together
4. Slice the onion and separate into rings
5. Grease your Ninja Foodi Grill with cooking spray
6. Then dip the onion rings into batter and coat with breadcrumbs

7. Arrange them in Ninja Foodi Grill Cooking Basket
8. Cook for 10 minutes
9. Serve and enjoy!

Nutrition:
- Calories: 450 kcal
- Carbs: 56 g
- Fat: 13 g.
- Protein: 30 g

4.7 Lemon-Garlic Shrimp Caesar Salad

Prep Time: 10 minutes
Cooking Time: 5 minutes
Servings: 4
Ingredients:
- 1-pound fresh jumbo shrimp
- 2 heads romaine lettuce, chopped
- 3/4 cup Caesar dressing
- 1/2 cup parmesan cheese, grated
- 1/2 lemon juice
- 3 garlic cloves, minced
- Sea salt
- Black pepper, grounded

Directions:
1. Addition the flame broils mesh and closes the hood. Pre-heat Ninja Foodi by pressing the "GRILL" option at and setting it to "MAX" and timer to 5 minutes

2. Take a large bowl; toss the shrimp with the lemon juice, garlic, salt, and pepper
3. Let it marinate while the grill is preheating
4. Once it pre-heat until you hear a beep
5. Arrange the shrimp over the grill grate lock lid and cook for 5 minutes
6. Toss the romaine lettuce with the Caesar dressing
7. Once cooked completely, remove the shrimp from the grill
8. Sprinkle with parmesan cheese
9. Serve and enjoy!

Nutrition:

- Calories: 279 kcal
- Carbs: 17 g
- Fat: 11 g.
- Protein: 30 g

4.8 Bacon Brussels Delight

Prep Time: 5-10 minutes
Cooking Time: 12 minutes
Servings: 4
Ingredients:

- 6 slices bacon, chopped
- 1-pound Brussels sprouts, halved
- 1/2 teaspoon black pepper
- 1 tablespoon of sea salt
- 2 tablespoons olive oil, extra-virgin

Directions:

1. Take a mixing bowl and toss the Brussels sprouts, olive oil, bacon, salt, and black pepper
2. Arrange the crisping basket inside the pot
3. Pre-heat Ninja Foodi by squeezing the "AIR CRISP" setting at 390 degrees F and timer to 12 minutes
4. Let it pre-heat until you hear a beep
5. Arrange the Brussels sprout mixture directly inside the basket
6. Close the top lid and cook for 6 minutes, then shake the basket
7. Close the top lid and cook for 6 minutes more
8. Serve warm and enjoy!

Nutrition:

- Calories: 279 kcal
- Carbs: 12.5 g
- Fat: 18.5 g.
- Protein: 14.5 g

4.9 Seared Tuna Salad

Prep Time: 10 minutes

Cooking Time: 6 minutes

Servings: 4

Ingredients:

- And 1/2-pounds ahi tuna, cut into four strips
- 2 tablespoons sesame oil
- 1(10 ounces) bag baby greens
- 2 tablespoons of rice wine vinegar
- 6 tablespoons extra-virgin olive oil

- 1/2 English cucumber, sliced
- 1/4 teaspoon of sea salt
- 1/2 teaspoon ground black pepper

Directions:

1. Supplement the flame broil mesh and close the hood
2. Pre-heat Ninja Foodi by pressing the "GRILL" option at and setting it to "MAX" and timer to 6 minutes
3. Take a small bowl, whisk together the rice vinegar, salt, and pepper
4. Slowly pour in the oil while whisking until vinaigrette is fully combined
5. Season the fish with salt and pepper, sprinkle with the sesame oil
6. Once it pre-heat until you hear a beep
7. Arrange the shrimp over the grill grate lock lid and cook for 6 minutes
8. Do not flip during cooking
9. Once cooked completely, top salad with tuna strip
10. Drizzle the vinaigrette over the top
11. Serve immediately and enjoy!

Nutrition:

- Calories: 427 kcal
- Carbs: 5 g
- Fat: 30 g.
- Protein: 36 g

4.10 Portobello and Pesto Sliders

Prep Time: 10 minutes

Cooking Time: 8 minutes

Servings: 4

Ingredients:

- 8 small Portobello mushrooms, trimmed with gills removed
- 1 tomato, sliced
- 2 tablespoons canola oil
- 1/2 cup pesto
- 1/2 cup micro greens
- 2 tablespoons balsamic vinegar
- 8 slider buns

Directions:

1. Addition the flame broils mesh and closes the hood
2. Pre-heat Ninja Foodi by pressing the "GRILL" option at and setting it to "HIGH" and timer to 8 minutes
3. Brush the mushrooms with oil and balsamic vinegar
4. Once it pre-heat until you hear a beep
5. Arrange the mushrooms over the grill grate lock lid and cook for 8 minutes
6. Once cooked, removed the mushrooms from the grill and layer on the buns with tomato, pesto, and micro greens
7. Serve immediately and enjoy!

Nutrition:

- Calories: 373 kcal
- Carbs: 33 g

- Fat: 22 g.
- Protein: 12 g

4.11 Crispy Rosemary Potatoes

Prep Time: 10 minutes
Cooking Time: 20 minutes
Servings: 4
Ingredients:

- 2 pounds baby red potatoes, quartered
- 2 tablespoons extra virgin olive oil
- 1/4 cup dried onion flakes
- 1/2 teaspoon onion powder
- 1/2 teaspoon garlic powder
- 1/4 teaspoon celery powder
- 1/4 teaspoon freshly ground black pepper
- 1/2 teaspoon dried parsley
- 1/2 teaspoon salt

Directions:

1. Take a large bowl and add all listed ingredients, toss well and coat them well
2. Pre-heat Ninja Foodi by squeezing the "AIR CRISP" alternative and setting it to "390 Degrees F" and clock to 20 minutes
3. Let it pre-heat until you hear a beep
4. Once preheated, add potatoes to the cooking basket
5. Lock and cook for 10 minutes, making sure to shake the basket and cook for 10 minutes more

6. Once done, check the crispiness, if it's alright, serve away.
7. If not, cook for 5 minutes more
8. Enjoy!

Nutrition:
- Calories: 232 kcal
- Carbs: 39 g
- Fat: 7 g.
- Protein: 4 g

4.12 Simple Crispy Brussels

Prep Time: 10 minutes
Cooking Time: 12 minutes
Servings: 4
Ingredients:
- 1-pound Brussels sprouts, halved
- 2 tablespoons olive oil, extra virgin
- 1/2 teaspoon ground black pepper
- 1 teaspoon salt
- 6 slices bacon, chopped

Directions:
1. Take a mixing bowl and add Brussels, olive oil, salt, pepper, and bacon
2. Pre-heat Ninja Foodi by squeezing the "AIR CRISP" alternative and setting it to "390 Degrees F and clock to 12 minutes
3. Let it pre-heat until you hear a beep
4. Arrange Brussels over basket and lock lid, cook for 6 minutes, shake and cook for 6 minutes more

5. Serve and enjoy!

Nutrition:

- Calories: 279 kcal
- Carbs: 12 g
- Fat: 18 g.
- Protein: 14 g

5. Delicious Poultry

5.1 Alfredo Flavored Apple Chicken

Prep Time: 5-10 minutes

Cooking Time: 20 minutes

Serving: 4

Ingredients:

- 1 large apple, wedged
- 1 tablespoon lemon juice
- 4 chicken breast, halved
- 4 teaspoon chicken seasoning
- 4 slices provolone cheese
- ¼ cup blue cheese, crumbled
- ½ cup alfredo sauce

Directions:

1. Take a bowl and add chicken, season it well
2. Take another bowl and add in apple, lemon juice
3. Preheat Ninja Foodi by pressing the "GRILL" option and setting it to "MED" and timer to 20 minutes
4. Let it preheat until you hear a beep
5. Arrange chicken over Grill Grate, lock lid and cook for 8 minutes, flip and cook for 8 minutes more
6. Grill apple in the same manner for 2 minutes per side (making sure to remove chicken beforehand)
7. Serve chicken with pepper, apple, blue cheese, and alfredo sauce
8. Enjoy!

Nutrition:

- Calories: 247
- Fat: 19 g
- Saturated Fat: 6 g
- Carbohydrates: 29 g
- Fiber: 6 g
- Sodium: 853 mg
- Protein: 14 g

5.2 Maple Flavored Chicken

Prep Time: 5-10 minutes

Cooking Time: 15 minutes

Serving: 4

Ingredients:

- 3 garlic cloves, minced
- 2 teaspoons garlic powder
- 2 teaspoons onion powder
- 1 teaspoon pepper
- ¼ cup teriyaki sauce
- 1 cup maple syrup
- 1/3 cup soy sauce
- 2 pounds bone-in chicken wings

Directions:

1. Take a mixing bowl and add soy sauce, pepper, onion powder, garlic, maple syrup, garlic powder, teriyaki sauce and combine well

2. Add chicken wings to the mixture and coat well
3. Preheat Ninja Foodi by pressing the "GRILL" option and setting it to "MED" and timer to 12 minutes
4. Let it preheat until you hear a beep
5. Arrange wings over grill grate and let it cook for 5 minutes, flip the wings and cook for 5 minutes more
6. Once the internal temperature reaches 165 degrees F, grill for 3-4 minutes more
7. Serve and enjoy!

Nutrition:

- Calories: 520
- Fat: 26 g
- Saturated Fat: 8 g
- Carbohydrates: 40 g
- Fiber: 3 g
- Sodium: 1400 mg
- Protein: 42 g

5.3 Classic Chicken Tomatina

Prep Time: 5-10 minutes

Cooking Time: 12 minutes

Serving: 4

Ingredients:

- 4 chicken breast, boneless and skinless
- ¼ cup fresh basil leaves
- 8 plum tomatoes

- 3/4 cup vinegar
- 2 tablespoons olive oil
- 1 garlic clove, minced
- ½ teaspoon salt

Directions:

1. Take your food processor and add basil, vinegar, olive oil, salt, garlic and blend until smooth
2. Add tomatoes and blend again
3. Take a mixing bowl and add chicken, tomato mixture and mix well, let it chill for 1-2 hours
4. Preheat Ninja Foodi by pressing the "GRILL" option and setting it to "HIGH" and timer to 6 minutes
5. Let it preheat until you hear a beep
6. Arrange prepared chicken over grill grate, lock lid and let it cook for 3 minutes
7. Flip chicken and cook for 3 minutes more, serve and enjoy!

Nutrition:

- Calories: 400
- Fat: 5 g
- Saturated Fat: 3 g
- Carbohydrates: 18 g
- Fiber: 3 g
- Sodium: 230 mg
- Protein: 23 g

5.4 Chicken Chili and Beans

Prep Time: 10 minutes

Cooking Time: 15 minutes

Serving: 4

Ingredients:

- 1 and ¼ pounds chicken breast, cut into pieces
- 1 can corn
- ¼ teaspoon garlic powder
- 1 can black beans, drained and rinsed
- 1 tablespoon oil
- 2 tablespoons chili powder
- 1 bell pepper, chopped
- ¼ teaspoon garlic powder
- ¼ teaspoon salt

Directions:

1. Pre-heat Ninja Foodi by pressing the "AIR CRISP" option and setting it to "360 Degrees F" and timer to 15 minutes
2. Place all the ingredients in your Ninja Foodi Grill cooking basket/alternatively, you may use a dish to mix the ingredients and then put the dish in the cooking basket
3. Stir to mix well
4. Cook for 15 minutes
5. **Serve and enjoy!**

Nutrition:

- Calories: 220
- Fat: 4 g

- Saturated Fat: 1 g
- Carbohydrates: 24 g
- Fiber: 2 g
- Sodium: 856 mg
- Protein: 20 g

5.5 Hearty Chicken Tomatina

Prep Time: 5-10 minutes
Cooking Time: 12 minutes
Serving: 4
Ingredients:

- 4 chicken breast, boneless and skinless
- ¼ cup fresh basil leaves
- 8 plum tomatoes
- 3/4 cup vinegar
- 2 tablespoons olive oil
- 1 garlic clove, minced
- ½ teaspoon salt

Directions:

8. Take your food processor and add basil, vinegar, olive oil, salt, garlic and blend until smooth
9. Add tomatoes and blend again
10. Take a mixing bowl and add chicken, tomato mixture and mix well, let it chill for 1-2 hours
11. Pre-heat Ninja Foodi by pressing the "GRILL" option and setting it to "HIGH" and timer to 12 minutes

12. Let it pre-heat until you hear a beep
13. Arrange prepared chicken over grill grate, lock lid and let it cook for 3 minutes
14. Flip chicken and cook for 3 minutes more, serve and enjoy!

Nutrition:

- Calories: 400
- Fat: 5 g
- Saturated Fat: 1 g
- Carbohydrates: 18 g
- Fiber: 3 g
- Sodium: 230 mg
- Protein: 23 g

5.6 Orange Flavored Chicken Fiesta

Prep Time: 5-10 minutes
Cooking Time: 10 minutes
Serving: 5
Ingredients:

- 2 teaspoons coriander, ground
- ½ teaspoon garlic salt
- ¼ teaspoon black pepper
- 12 chicken wings
- 1 tablespoon canola oil

Sauce

- ¼ cup butter
- 3 tablespoons honey

- ½ cup orange juice
- 1/3 cup Sriracha chili sauce
- 2 tablespoons lime juice
- ¼ cup cilantro, chopped

Directions:

1. Take your chicken and coat with oil, season well with spices and let it chill for 2 hours
2. Take a bowl and add sauce ingredients, mix well. Stir cook for 3-4 minutes
3. Set you Ninja Foodi to GRILL mode and select MED, adjust the timer to 10 minutes
4. Let it preheat until you hear a beep
5. Arrange chicken over grill, lock lid and cook for 5 minutes, flip and cook for 5 minutes more
6. Serve and enjoy!

Nutrition:

- Calories: 327
- Fat: 14 g
- Saturated Fat: 3 g
- Carbohydrates: 19 g
- Fiber: 1 g
- Sodium: 258 mg
- Protein: 25 g

5.7 Thai Baked Soy Chicken

Prep Time: 5-10 minutes

Cooking Time: 25 minutes

Serving: 5

Ingredients:

- ½ cup of soy sauce
- ¼ cup apple cider vinegar
- 1 garlic clove, minced
- 1 tablespoon cornstarch
- 1 tablespoon cold water
- ½ cup white sugar
- ¼ teaspoon ground pepper
- ½ teaspoon ground ginger
- 12 skinless chicken thighs

Directions:

1. Take a mixing bowl and add cornstarch water, white sugar, soy sauce, apple cider, vinegar, garlic, ginger, and pepper, mix and combine well
2. Season chicken with salt and pepper
3. Take your cooking pan and grease well with oil, add chicken and soy sauce mix on top
4. Preheat Ninja Foodi by pressing the "BAKE" option and setting it to "350 degrees F" and timer to 25 minutes
5. Let it preheat until you hear a beep
6. Arrange the pan over grill grate, lock lid and let it cook until the timer goes to zero
7. Serve and enjoy!

Nutrition:

- Calories: 570
- Fat: 19 g
- Saturated Fat: 5 g
- Carbohydrates: 23 g
- Fiber: 1 g
- Sodium: 600 mg
- Protein: 40 g

5.8 Seasoned Turkey Cutlets

Prep Time: 5-10 min.

Cooking Time: 22 min.

Serving: 4

Ingredients:

- 2 tablespoons olive oil
- 1 teaspoon turmeric powder
- ½ cup almond flour
- 1 teaspoon Greek seasoning
- 1 pound turkey cutlets

Directions:

1. In a mixing bowl, add the Greek seasoning, turmeric powder, and almond flour. Combine the ingredients to mix well with each other. Add the turkey cutlets and coat well; set aside for 30 minutes.
2. Take Ninja Foodi multi-cooker, arrange it over a cooking platform, and open the top lid.
3. In the pot, add the oil; Select "SEAR/SAUTÉ" mode and select "MD: HI" pressure level. Press "STOP/START." After about 4-5 minutes, the oil will start simmering.

4. Add the cutlets and stir-cook for about 2-3 minutes to brown evenly.
5. Seal the multi-cooker by locking it with the pressure lid; ensure to keep the pressure release valve locked/sealed.
6. Select "PRESSURE" mode and select the "LOW: MD" pressure level. Then, set timer to 20 minutes and press "STOP/START"; it will start the cooking process by building up inside pressure.
7. When the timer goes off, naturally release inside pressure for about 8-10 minutes. Then, quick-release pressure by adjusting the pressure valve to the VENT. Serve warm.

Nutrition:

- Calories: 355
- Fat: 18.5g
- Saturated Fat: 1g
- Trans Fat: 0g
- Carbohydrates: 4g
- Fiber: 0.5g
- Sodium: 544mg
- Protein: 35g

5.9 Soy Flavored Thai Chicken

Prep Time: 5-10 minutes

Cooking Time: 25 minutes

Serving: 5

Ingredients:

- ½ cup of soy sauce
- ¼ cup apple cider vinegar
- 1 garlic clove, minced

- 1 tablespoon cornstarch
- 1 tablespoon cold water
- ½ cup white sugar
- ¼ teaspoon ground pepper
- ½ teaspoon ground ginger
- 12 skinless chicken thighs

Directions:

1. Take a mixing bowl and add cornstarch water, white sugar, soy sauce, apple cider, vinegar, garlic, ginger, and pepper, mix and combine well
2. Season chicken with salt and pepper
3. Take your cooking pan and grease well with oil, add chicken and soy sauce mix on top
4. Preheat Ninja Foodi by pressing the "BAKE" option and setting it to "350 degrees F" and timer to 25 minutes
5. Let it preheat until you hear a beep
6. Arrange the pan over grill grate, lock lid and let it cook until the timer goes to zero
7. Serve and enjoy!

Nutrition:

- Calories: 570
- Fat: 19 g
- Saturated Fat: 5 g
- Carbohydrates: 23 g
- Fiber: 1 g
- Sodium: 600 mg
- Protein: 40 g

5.10 Tomato and Turkey Meal

Prep Time: 10 minutes

Cooking Time: 40 minutes

Serving: 4

Ingredients:

- 3 ounces plain granola
- 2 pounds lean turkey, grounded
- 6 burger buns of your choice, sliced in half
- 2/3 cup sun-dried tomatoes, chopped
- 1 cup feta cheese, crumbled
- ¼ teaspoon salt
- ¼ teaspoon pepper
- 1 large red onion, chopped

Directions:

1. Take a mixing bowl, add all the ingredients and combine them well
2. Prepare six patties from the mixture
3. Arrange the grill grate and close the lid
4. Preheat Ninja Foodi by pressing the "GRILL" option and setting it to "MED" and timer to 14 minutes
5. Let it preheat until you hear a beep
6. Arrange the patties over the grill grate, lock lid and cook for 7 minutes more
7. Serve warm with ciabatta rolls and your favorite toppings
8. Enjoy!

Nutrition:

- Calories: 298
- Fat: 16 g

- Saturated Fat: 4 g
- Carbohydrates: 32 g
- Fiber: 4 g
- Sodium: 168 mg
- Protein: 27 g

5.12 Zucchini and Chicken Kabobs

Prep Time: 10 minutes

Cooking Time: 15 minutes

Serving: 4

Ingredients:

- 1 pound chicken breast, boneless, skinless and cut into cubes of 2 inches
- 2 tablespoons Greek yogurt, plain
- 4 lemons juice
- 1 lemon zest
- ¼ cup extra-virgin olive oil
- 2 tablespoons oregano
- 1 red onion, quartered
- 1 zucchini, sliced
- 4 garlic cloves, minced
- 1 teaspoon of sea salt
- ½ teaspoon ground black pepper

Directions:

1. Take a mixing bowl, add the Greek yogurt, lemon juice, oregano, garlic, zest, salt, and pepper, combine them well

2. Add the chicken and coat well, refrigerate for 1-2 hours to marinate
3. Arrange the grill grate and close the lid
4. Preheat Ninja Foodi by pressing the "GRILL" option and setting it to "MED" and timer to 7 minutes
5. Take the skewers, thread the chicken, zucchini and red onion and thread alternatively
6. Let it preheat until you hear a beep
7. Arrange the skewers over the grill grate, lock lid and cook until the timer reads zero
8. Baste the kebabs with a marinating mixture in between
9. Take out your when it reaches 165 degrees F
10. Serve warm and enjoy!

Nutrition:

- Calories: 277
- Fat: 15 g
- Saturated Fat: 4 g
- Carbohydrates: 10 g
- Fiber: 2 g
- Sodium: 146 mg
- Protein: 25 g

6. Fish & Seafood

6.1 Coconut Baked Trout

Prep Time: 5-10 minutes

Cooking Time: 15 minutes

Servings: 4

Ingredients:

- 2 tablespoons parsley, chopped
- 2 teaspoons olive oil
- 2 teaspoons garlic, minced
- 4 trout fillets, skinless and boneless
- 1/2 cup coconut milk
- Black pepper (ground) and salt to taste

Directions:

1. Take a baking pan, grease it with some cooking spray, vegetable oil, or butter. Add all the ingredients and combine well.
2. Take Ninja Foodi multi-cooker, arrange it over a cooking platform, and open the top lid.
3. In the pot, add water and place a reversible rack inside the pot. Place the pan over the rack.
4. Seal the multi-cooker by locking it with the Crisping Lid, ensure to keep the pressure release valve locked/sealed.
5. Select "BAKE/ROAST" mode and adjust the 380°F temperature level. Then after, set timer to 15 minutes and press "STOP/START," it will start the cooking process by building up inside pressure.

6. When the timer goes off, quickly release pressure by adjusting the pressure valve to the VENT. After pressure gets released, open the Crisping Lid. Serve warm.

Nutrition:

- Calories: 320
- Fat: 16g
- Saturated Fat: 4g
- Trans Fat: 0g
- Carbohydrates: 17g
- Fiber: 2.5g
- Sodium: 954mg
- Protein: 28.5g

6.2 Shrimp Pie Meal

Prep Time: 5-10 minutes
Cooking Time: 18 minutes
Servings: 6
Ingredients:

- 1 celery stalk, diced
- 1 carrot, peeled and diced
- ¼ cup unsalted butter
- ½ large onion, diced
- 16 ounces shrimp, cleaned, tailed removed, and deveined
- ¾ cup chicken stock
- 8 ounces chorizo, fully cooked, cut into ½-inch rounds
- ¼ cup all-purpose flour

- 1 tablespoon Cajun spice mix
- ½ cup heavy (whipping) cream
- 1 refrigerated store-bought pie crust
- Sea salt
- Black pepper (ground)

Directions:

1. Take Ninja Foodi multi-cooker, arrange it over a cooking platform, and open the top lid.
2. In the pot, add the butter, Select "SEAR/SAUTÉ" mode and select "MD: HI" pressure level. Press "STOP/START." After about 4-5 minutes, the butter will melt.
3. Add the onions, celery, carrot, and sausage and cook (while stirring) until they become softened and translucent for 3 minutes.
4. Mix the flour and cook 2 minutes. Add the shrimp, stock, Cajun spice mix, cream, salt and pepper, stir cook for 3 minutes.
5. In the pie crust, add the filling mixture and fold the edges. Make cuts on top for steam escape. Add the pie in the pot.
6. Seal the multi-cooker by locking it with the Crisping Lid, ensure to keep the pressure release valve locked/sealed.
7. Select "BROIL" mode and select the "HI" pressure level. Then after, set timer to 10 minutes and press "STOP/START," it will start the cooking process by building up inside pressure.
8. When the timer goes off, quickly release pressure by adjusting the pressure valve to the VENT. After pressure gets released, open the Crisping Lid. Serve warm.

Nutrition:

- Calories: 479
- Fat: 32.5g
- Saturated Fat: 12g

- Trans Fat: 0g
- Carbohydrates: 18g
- Fiber: 1.5g

6.3 Juicy Rosemary Garlic Salmon

Prep Time: 5-10 minutes
Cooking Time: 12 minutes
Servings: 3
Ingredients:

- ¼ teaspoon pepper
- 1 garlic clove, minced
- ¼ teaspoon salt
- ¼ teaspoon fresh rosemary, minced
- 1 teaspoon lemon zest, grated
- 2 salmon fillets, 6 ounces each

Directions:

1. Take a mixing bowl and add all listed ingredients except salmon, mix well
2. Add salmon and combine, let it sit for 15 minutes
3. Pre-heat Ninja Foodi by pressing the "GRILL" option and setting it to "MED" and timer to 6 minutes
4. Let it pre-heat until you hear a beep
5. Arrange salmon over grill grate, lock lid and cook for 3 minutes
6. Flip and cook for 3 minutes more, serve and enjoy!

Nutrition:

- Calories: 250

- Fat: 8 g
- Saturated Fat: 3g
- Carbohydrates: 22 g
- Fiber: 3 g
- Sodium: 370 mg
- Protein: 36 g

6.4 Mustard Crispy Cod

Prep Time: 5-10 minutes
Cooking Time: 10 minutes
Servings: 3
Ingredients:

- 1 large whole egg
- 1 teaspoon Dijon mustard
- ½ cup breadcrumbs
- 1-pound cod filets
- ¼ cup all-purpose flour
- 1 tablespoon dried parsley
- 1 teaspoon paprika
- ½ teaspoon pepper

Directions:

1. Take fish filets and cut them into 1-inch wide strips
2. Take a blending bowl and speed in eggs, include mustard and consolidate well
3. Include flour in another bowl

4. Take another bowl and include breadcrumbs, dried parsley, paprika, dark pepper and join well
5. Coat strips with flour, at that point cover with egg blend, and cover with scraps finally
6. Pre-heat Ninja Foodi by squeezing the "AIR CRISP" alternative and setting it to "390 Degrees F" and clock to 10 minutes
7. Let it pre-heat until you hear a beep
8. Arrange strips directly inside basket, lock lid and cook until the timer runs out
9. Serve and enjoy!

Nutrition:

- Calories: 200
- Fat: 4 g
- Saturated Fat: 1 g
- Carbohydrates: 17 g
- Fiber: 1 g
- Sodium: 214 mg
- Protein: 24 g

6.5 Buttery Spiced Grilled Salmon

Prep Time: 5-10 minutes

Cooking Time: 10 minutes

Servings: 4

Ingredients:

- 2 teaspoons cayenne pepper
- 2 pounds salmon fillets
- 2 teaspoon salt

- 6 tablespoons butter, melted
- 1 and ¼ teaspoon onion salt
- 2 tablespoons lemon pepper
- 1 teaspoon white pepper, ground
- 1 teaspoon black pepper, ground
- 1 teaspoon dry basil
- 1 teaspoon ancho chili powder
- 1 teaspoon dry oregano
- Lemon wedges and dill sprigs

Directions:

1. Season salmon fillets with butter, take a mixing bowl and add listed ingredients
2. Coat salmon fillets with the mixture
3. Pre-heat Ninja Foodi by pressing the "GRILL" option and setting it to "MED" and timer to 10 minutes
4. Let it pre-heat until you hear a beep
5. Arrange prepared fillets over grill grate, let them cook for 5 minutes, flip and cook for 5 minutes more
6. Serve and enjoy!

Nutrition:

- Calories: 300
- Fat: 8 g   Saturated Fat: 2 g
- Carbohydrates: 17 g
- Fiber: 1 g
- Sodium: 342 mg
- Protein: 26 g

6.6 Crispy Crabby Patties

Prep Time: 5-10 minutes

Cooking Time: 10 minutes

Servings: 4

Ingredients:

- 1 shallot, minced
- ¼ cup mayonnaise, low carb
- 12 ounces lump crabmeat
- ¼ cup parsley, minced
- 2 tablespoons Dijon mustard
- 2 tablespoons almond flour
- 1 lemon, zest
- 1 egg, beaten
- Pepper and salt as needed

Directions:

1. Take a mixing bowl and add all ingredients, mix well and prepare 4 meat from the mixture
2. Pre-heat Ninja Foodi by squeezing the "AIR CRISP" choice and setting it to "375 Degrees F" and timer to 10 minutes
3. Let it pre-heat until you hear a beep
4. Transfer patties to cooking basket and let them cook for 5 minutes, flip and cook for 5 minutes more
5. Serve and enjoy once done!

Nutrition:

- Calories: 177
- Fat: 13 g

- Saturated Fat: 2 g
- Carbohydrates: 2.5 g
- Fiber: 0 g
- Sodium: 358 mg
- Protein: 11 g

6.7 Spicy Grilled Shrimps

Prep Time: 5-10 minutes
Cooking Time: 6 minutes
Servings: 4
Ingredients:

- 1 teaspoon garlic salt
- ½ teaspoon black pepper
- 1 tablespoon paprika
- 1 tablespoon garlic powder
- 2 tablespoons olive oil
- 1-pound jumbo shrimps, peeled and deveined
- 2 tablespoons brown sugar

Directions:

1. Take a mixing bowl and add listed ingredients to mix well
2. Let it chill and marinate for 30-60 minutes
3. Pre-heat Ninja Foodi by pressing the "GRILL" option and setting it to "MED" and timer to 6 minutes
4. Let it pre-heat until you hear a beep
5. Arrange prepared shrimps over grill grate, lock lid and cook for 3 minutes, flip and cook for 3 minutes more

6. Serve and enjoy!

Nutrition:

- Calories: 370
- Fat: 27 g
- Saturated Fat: 3 g
- Carbohydrates: 23 g
- Fiber: 8 g
- Sodium: 182 mg
- Protein: 6 g

6.8 Baked Parmesan Fish

Prep Time: 5-10 minutes
Cooking Time: 13 minutes
Servings: 3
Ingredients:

- ¼ teaspoon salt
- ¾ cup breadcrumbs
- ¼ cup parmesan cheese, grated
- ¼ teaspoon ground dried thyme
- ¼ cup butter, melted
- 1-pound haddock fillets
- ¾ cup milk

Directions:

1. Coat fish fillets in milk, season with salt and keep it on the side
2. Take a mixing bowl and add breadcrumbs, parmesan, cheese, thyme and combine well

3. Coat fillets in bread crumb mixture
4. Pre-heat Ninja Foodi by pressing the "BAKE" option and setting it to "325 Degrees F" and timer to 13 minutes
5. Let it pre-heat until you hear a beep
6. Arrange fish fillets directly over Grill Grate, lock lid and cook for 8 minutes, flip and cook for the remaining time
7. Serve and enjoy!

Nutrition:

- Calories: 450
- Fat: 27 g
- Saturated Fat: 12 g
- Carbohydrates: 16 g
- Fiber: 22 g
- Sodium: 1056 mg
- Protein: 44 g

6.9 Roast BBQ Shrimp

Prep Time: 5-10 minutes
Cooking Time: 7 minutes
Servings: 2
Ingredients:

- 3 tablespoons chipotle in adobo sauce, minced
- ¼ teaspoon salt
- ¼ cup BBQ sauce
- ½ orange, juiced
- ½ pound large shrimps

Directions:

1. Take a mixing bowl and add all ingredients, mix well
2. Keep it on the side
3. Pre-heat Ninja Foodi by pressing the "ROAST" option and setting it to "400 Degrees F" and timer to 7 minutes
4. Let it pre-heat until you hear a beep
5. Arrange shrimps over Grill Grate and lock lid, cook until the timer runs out
6. Serve and enjoy!

Nutrition:

- Calories: 173
- Fat: 2 g
- Saturated Fat: 0.5 g
- Carbohydrates: 21 g
- Fiber: 2 g
- Sodium: 1143 mg
- Protein: 17 g

6.10 Wholesome Broccoli Shrimp

Prep Time: 5-10 minutes

Cooking Time: 2 minutes

Servings: 4

Ingredients:

- 3 garlic cloves, minced
- ¼ cup white wine
- 2 tablespoons unsalted butter

- 1 shallot, minced
- ½ cup chicken stock
- ½ teaspoon Black pepper (ground)
- 1 ½ pounds frozen shrimp, thawed
- Juice of ½ lemon
- ½ teaspoon of sea salt
- 1 large head broccoli, cut into florets

Directions:

1. Take Ninja Foodi multi-cooker, arrange it over a cooking platform, and open the top lid.
2. In the pot, add the butter, select "SEAR/SAUTÉ" mode and select "MD: HI" pressure level. Press "STOP/START." After about 4-5 minutes, the butter will melt.
3. Add the shallots and cook (while stirring) until they become softened and translucent for 2-3 minutes.
4. Add the garlic and cook for 1 minute. Add the wine and stir gently. Mix in the chicken stock, lemon juice, salt, pepper, broccoli, and shrimp.
5. Seal the multi-cooker by locking it with the pressure lid, ensure to keep the pressure release valve locked/sealed.
6. Select "PRESSURE" mode and select the "HI" pressure level. Then after, set timer to 1 minute and press "STOP/START," it will start the cooking process by building up inside pressure.
7. When the timer goes off, quickly release pressure by adjusting the pressure valve to the VENT. After pressure gets released, open the pressure lid. Serve warm.

Nutrition:

- Calories: 286
- Fat: 7.5g
- Saturated Fat: 3.5g

- Trans Fat: 0g
- Carbohydrates: 10g
- Fiber: 3g
- Sodium: 657mg
- Protein: 38g

6.11 Creamed Salmon

Prep Time: 5-10 minutes
Cooking Time: 14 minutes
Servings: 4
Ingredients:

- 2 garlic cloves, minced
- 2 tablespoons butter, melted
- 1 tablespoon chives, chopped
- 1-pound salmon, boneless, skinless and cubed
- 1/4 cup heavy cream
- Black pepper (ground) and salt to taste

Directions:

1. Take Ninja Foodi multi-cooker, arrange it over a cooking platform, and open the top lid.
2. In the pot, add the butter, select "SEAR/SAUTÉ" mode and select "MD: HI" pressure level. Press "STOP/START." After about 4-5 minutes, the butter will melt.
3. Add the chives, garlic, and cook (while stirring) until they become softened for 2 minutes.
4. Add remaining ingredients, stir gently.

5. Seal the multi-cooker by locking it with the pressure lid, ensure to keep the pressure release valve locked/sealed.
6. Select "PRESSURE" mode and select the "HI" pressure level. Then after, set timer to 12 minutes and press "STOP/START," it will start the cooking process by building up inside pressure.
7. When the timer goes off, naturally release inside pressure for about 8-10 minutes. Then, quick-release pressure by adjusting the pressure valve to the VENT. Serve warm.

Nutrition:

- Calories: 286
- Fat: 19g
- Saturated Fat: 9g
- Trans Fat: 0g
- Carbohydrates: 2g
- Fiber: 0g
- Sodium: 930mg
- Protein: 24g

6.12 Cream Mussels with Bread

Prep Time: 5-10 minutes

Cooking Time: 25 minutes

Servings: 4

Ingredients:

- 3 garlic cloves, minced
- 1 cup cherry tomatoes, halved
- 2 tablespoons vegetable oil
- 2 shallots, sliced

- 2 cups heavy cream
- 1 ½ teaspoons cayenne pepper
- 1 ½ teaspoon Black pepper (ground)
- 2 pounds mussels, scrubbed and debearded
- 2 cups white wine
- 1 loaf sourdough bread, cut into slices

Directions:

1. Take Ninja Foodi multi-cooker, arrange it over a cooking platform, and open the top lid.
2. In the pot, add the oil, select "SEAR/SAUTÉ" mode and select "MD: HI" pressure level. Press "STOP/START." After about 4-5 minutes, the oil will start simmering.
3. Add the shallots, garlic, and cherry tomatoes and cook (while stirring) until they become softened and translucent for 4-5 minutes.
4. Add the mussels, wine, heavy cream, cayenne, black pepper, stir gently.
5. Seal the multi-cooker by locking it with the pressure lid, ensure to keep the pressure release valve locked/sealed.
6. Select the "STEAM" mode and select the "HI" pressure level. Then after, set timer to 20 minutes and press "STOP/START," it will start the cooking process by building up inside pressure.
7. When the timer goes off, quickly release pressure by adjusting the pressure valve to the VENT. After pressure gets released, open the pressure lid. Serve warm with bread.

Nutrition:

- Calories: 842
- Fat: 26g
- Saturated Fat: 13g
- Trans Fat: 0g

- Carbohydrates: 56g
- Fiber: 3.5g
- Sodium: 1123mg
- Protein: 39g

6.13 Cod Sandwich

Prep Time: 5-10 minutes
Cooking Time: 15 minutes
Servings: 4
Ingredients:

- 1 cup cornstarch
- 1 cup all-purpose flour
- 2 eggs
- 8 ounces ale
- 1 teaspoon sea salt
- 1 teaspoon black pepper (ground)
- ½ tablespoon chili powder
- 1 tablespoon ground cumin
- Tartar sauce
- 8 slices sandwich bread
- 4 (5-6 ounce) cod fillets, cut into 16 half-inch strips

Directions:

1. In a blending bowl, whisk the eggs and beer. In another bowl, whisk the cornstarch, flour, chili powder, cumin, salt, and pepper.
2. First, coat the cod fillets with the egg mixture and then with the flour mixture.

3. Take Ninja Foodi multi-cooker, arrange it over a cooking platform, and open the top lid.

4. In the pot, place the Crisping Basket, coat it with some cooking oil. In the basket, add the fillets.

5. Seal the multi-cooker by locking it with the crisping lid, ensure to keep the pressure release valve locked/sealed.

6. Select the "AIR CRISP" mode and adjust the 375°F temperature level. Then after, set timer to 15 minutes and press "STOP/START," it will start the cooking process by building up inside pressure.

7. When the timer goes off, quickly release pressure by adjusting the pressure valve to the VENT. After pressure gets released, open the Crisping Lid.

8. Arrange four bread slices and spread the tartar sauce over, place the fillets, and add remaining slices on top. Serve fresh.

Nutrition:

- Calories: 511
- Fat: 12.5g
- Saturated Fat: 2g
- Trans Fat: 0g
- Carbohydrates: 56.5g
- Fiber: 3g
- Sodium: 1147mg
- Protein: 36g

6.14 Classic Honey Salmon

Prep Time: 5-10 minutes

Cooking Time: 10 minutes

Servings: 4

Ingredients:

- 1 tablespoon olive oil
- 2 tablespoons honey
- 1-pound salmon fillets, boneless, skinless and cubed
- 1/4 cup lime juice
- Black pepper (ground) and salt to taste

Directions:

1. Take Ninja Foodi multi-cooker, arrange it over a cooking platform, and open the top lid.
2. In the pot, add the oil, salmon, and other ingredients. Stir gently.
3. Seal the multi-cooker by locking it with the pressure lid, ensure to keep the pressure release valve locked/sealed.
4. Select "PRESSURE" mode and select the "HI" pressure level. Then after, set timer to 10 minutes and press "STOP/START," it will start the cooking process by building up inside pressure.
5. When the timer goes off, naturally release inside pressure for about 8-10 minutes. Then, quick-release pressure by adjusting the pressure valve to the VENT. Serve warm.

Nutrition:

- Calories: 268
- Fat: 13g
- Saturated Fat: 1g
- Trans Fat: 0g

- Carbohydrates: 9g
- Fiber: 0.5g
- Sodium: 936mg
- Protein: 29g

6.15 Sausage Potato Shrimp

Prep Time: 5-10 minutes
Cooking Time: 10 minutes
Servings: 6
Ingredients:

- 1 (14-ounce) package smoked sausage or kielbasa, sliced into 1-inch pieces
- 4 cups water
- 2 pounds red potatoes, diced
- 3 ears corn, cut crosswise into thirds
- 2 ½ tablespoons Creole seasoning
- 1-pound medium (21–30 count) shrimp, peeled and deveined

Directions:

1. Take Ninja Foodi multi-cooker, arrange it over a cooking platform, and open the top lid.
2. In the pot, add the potatoes, corn, sausage, water, and Creole seasoning. Stir gently.
3. Seal the multi-cooker by locking it with the pressure lid, ensure to keep the pressure release valve locked/sealed.
4. Select "PRESSURE" mode and select the "HI" pressure level. Then after, set timer to 5 minutes and press "STOP/START," it will start the cooking process by building up inside pressure.

5. When the timer goes off, quickly release pressure by adjusting the pressure valve to the VENT. After pressure gets released, open the pressure lid.
6. Select "SEAR/SAUTÉ" mode and select the "LO" pressure level, add the shrimps and combine. Stir-cook for 4-5 minutes. Serve warm.

Nutrition:

- Calories: 426
- Fat: 18g
- Saturated Fat: 5.5g
- Trans Fat: 0g
- Carbohydrates: 37.5g
- Fiber: 6g
- Sodium: 987mg
- Protein: 37.5g

6.16 Crispy Garlic Mackerel

Prep Time: 5-10 minutes

Cooking Time: 12 minutes

Servings: 4

Ingredients:

- 1 teaspoon garlic powder
- 1 teaspoon cumin, ground
- 4 mackerel fillets, boneless
- 1 tablespoon canola oil
- Juice of 1 lime
- Black pepper (ground) and salt to taste

Directions:

1. Take Ninja Foodi multi-cooker, arrange it over a cooking platform, and open the top lid.
2. In the pot, arrange a reversible rack and place the Crisping Basket over the rack. In the basket, add the fish and other ingredients, combine well.
3. Seal the multi-cooker by locking it with the crisping lid, ensure to keep the pressure release valve locked/sealed.
4. Select the "AIR CRISP" mode and adjust the 370°F temperature level. Then after, set timer to 12 minutes and press "STOP/START," it will start the cooking process by building up inside pressure. Flip the fish after 6 minutes.
5. When the timer goes off, quickly release pressure by adjusting the pressure valve to the VENT. After pressure gets released, open the Crisping Lid. Serve warm with chopped salad greens (optional).

Nutrition:

- Calories: 411
- Fat: 31.5g
- Saturated Fat: 8g
- Trans Fat: 0g
- Carbohydrates: 8g
- Fiber: 1g
- Sodium: 1025mg
- Protein: 22g

7. Pork, Beef & Lamb

7.1 Kale Sausage Soup

Prep Time: 5-10 minutes

Cooking Time: 10 minutes

Servings: 4

Ingredients:

- ½ diced onion
- 2 cup chicken broth
- 1-pound chopped sausage roll
- 1 tablespoon olive oil
- 2 cup almond milk
- ½ cup parmesan cheese
- 3 cup chopped kale fresh
- 28-ounce tomatoes, crushed
- 1 tablespoon minced garlic
- 1 teaspoon oregano, dried
- ¼ teaspoon salt

Directions:

1. Take Ninja Foodi multi-cooker, arrange it over a cooking platform, and open the top lid.
2. Select "SEAR/SAUTÉ" mode and select "MD: HI" pressure level. Press "STOP/START." After about 4-5 minutes, the unit is ready to cook.
3. Add the sausage and stir-cook to brown evenly. Add the spices, onions, kale, tomatoes, milk, and chicken broth. Stir the mixture.

4. Seal the multi-cooker by locking it with the pressure lid; ensure to keep the pressure release valve locked/sealed.
5. Select "PRESSURE" mode and select the "HI" pressure level. Then, set timer to 10 minutes and press "STOP/START"; it will start the cooking process by building up inside pressure.
6. When the timer goes off, naturally release inside pressure for about 8-10 minutes. Then, quick-release pressure by adjusting the pressure valve to the VENT. Serve warm with the cheese on top and enjoy!

Nutrition:

- Calories: 162
- Fat: 10.5g
- Saturated Fat: 4g
- Trans Fat: 0g
- Carbohydrates: 2g
- Fiber: 0.5g
- Sodium: 624mg
- Protein: 19g

7.2 Spinach Beef Meatloaf

Prep Time: 5-10 minutes

Cooking Time: 70 minutes

Servings: 6

Ingredients:

- ¼ cup tomato puree or crushed tomatoes
- 1-pound lean ground beef
- ½ cup onion, chopped
- 2 garlic cloves, minced

- ½ cup green bell pepper, seeded and chopped
- 2 eggs, beaten
- 1 cup cheddar cheese, grated
- 3 cups spinach, chopped
- 1 teaspoon dried thyme, crushed
- 6 cups mozzarella cheese, grated
- Black pepper to taste

Directions:

1. Take a baking pan; grease it with some cooking spray, vegetable oil, or butter. Take Ninja Foodi multi-cooker, arrange it over a cooking platform, and open the top lid.
2. In a blending bowl, include the entirety of the listed ingredients except cheese and spinach.
3. Place the mixture over a wax paper; top with spinach, cheese, and roll it to form a nice meatloaf. Remove wax paper and add the mixture in the baking pan.
4. In the pot, add water and place a reversible rack inside the pot. Place the pan over the rack.
5. Seal the multi-cooker by locking it with the crisping lid; ensure to keep the pressure release valve locked/sealed.
6. Select "BAKE/ROAST" mode and adjust the 380°F temperature level. Then, set timer to 70 minutes and press "STOP/START"; it will start the cooking process by building up inside pressure.
7. At the point when the clock goes off, fast discharge pressure by adjusting the pressure valve to the VENT. After pressure gets released, open the pressure lid.
8. Serve warm.

Nutrition:

- Calories: 426

- Fat: 16.5g
- Saturated Fat: 2g
- Trans Fat: 0g
- Carbohydrates: 5.5g
- Fiber: 1g
- Sodium: 743mg
- Protein: 48.5g

7.3 Steak Pineapple Mania

Prep Time: 5-10 minutes
Cooking Time: 8 minutes
Servings: 4-5
Ingredients:

- ½ medium pineapple, cored and diced
- 1 jalapeño pepper, seeded, stemmed, and diced
- 1 medium red onion, diced
- 4 (6-8-ounce) filet mignon steaks
- 1 tablespoon canola oil
- Sea salt and ground black pepper to taste
- 1 tablespoon lime juice
- ¼ cup chopped cilantro leaves
- Chili powder and ground coriander to taste

Directions:

1. Rub the fillets with the oil evenly, then season with the salt and black pepper.

2. Take Ninja Foodi Grill, arrange it over your kitchen platform, and open the top lid.
3. Arrange the grill grate and close the top lid.
4. Press "GRILL" and select the "HIGH" grill function. Adjust the timer to 8 minutes and then press "START/STOP." Ninja Foodi will start preheating.
5. Ninja Foodi is preheated and ready to cook when it starts to beep. After you hear a beep, open the top lid.
6. Arrange the fillets over the grill grate. Close the top lid and cook for 4 minutes. Now open the top lid, flip the fillets.
7. Close the top lid and cook for 4 more minutes. Cook until the food thermometer reaches 125°F.
8. In a mixing bowl, add the pineapple, onion, and jalapeño. Combine well. Add the lime juice, cilantro, chili powder, and coriander. Combine again.
9. Serve the fillets warm with the pineapple mixture on top.

Nutrition:
- Calories: 536
- Fat: 22.5g
- Saturated Fat: 7g
- Trans Fat: 0g
- Carbohydrates: 21g
- Fiber: 4g
- Sodium: 286mg
- Protein: 58g

7.4 Avocado Salsa Steak

Prep Time: 5-10 minutes

Cooking Time: 18 minutes

Servings: 4

Ingredients:

- 1 cup cilantro leaves
- 2 ripe avocados, diced
- 2 cups salsa Verde
- 2 beef flank steak, diced
- 1/2 teaspoon salt
- 1/2 teaspoon pepper
- 2 medium tomatoes, seeded and diced

Directions:

1. Rub the beef steak with salt and black pepper to season well.
2. Take Ninja Foodi Grill, orchestrate it over your kitchen stage, and open the top cover.
3. Orchestrate the flame broil mesh and close the top cover.
4. Press "Barbecue" and select the "MED" flame broil work. Alter the clock to 18 minutes and afterward press "START/STOP." Ninja Foodi will begin pre-warming.
5. Ninja Foodi is preheated and prepared to cook when it begins to signal. After you hear a blare, open the top. Arrange the diced steak over the grill grate.
6. Close the top lid and cook for 9 minutes. Now open the top lid, flip the diced steak.
7. Close the top lid and cook for 9 more minutes.
8. In a blender, blend the salsa and cilantro. Serve the grilled steak with the blended salsa, tomato, and avocado.

Nutrition:

- Calories: 523
- Fat: 31.5g
- Saturated Fat: 9g
- Trans Fat: 0g
- Carbohydrates: 38.5g
- Fiber: 2g
- Sodium: 301mg
- Protein: 41.5g

7.5 Bourbon Pork Chops

Prep Time: 5-10 minutes

Cooking Time: 20 minutes

Servings: 4

Ingredients:

- 4 boneless pork chops
- Ocean salt and ground dark pepper to taste
- ¼ cup apple cider vinegar
- ¼ cup soy sauce
- 3 tablespoons Worcestershire sauce
- 2 cups ketchup
- ¾ cup bourbon
- 1 cup packed brown sugar
- ½ tablespoon dry mustard powder

Directions:

1. Take Ninja Foodi Grill, orchestrate it over your kitchen stage, and open the top cover. Orchestrate the flame broil mesh and close the top cover.
2. Click "GRILL" and choose the "MED" grill function. Adjust the timer to 15 minutes and click "START/STOP."
3. Ninja Foodi is preheated and prepared to cook when it begins to signal. After you hear a signal, open the top.
4. Arrange the pork chops over the grill grate.
5. Close the top lid and cook for 8 minutes. Now open the top lid, flip the pork chops.
6. Close the top lid and cook for 8 more minutes. Check the pork chops for doneness, cook for 2 more minutes if required.
7. In a saucepan, heat the soy sauce, sugar, ketchup, bourbon, vinegar, Worcestershire sauce, and mustard powder; stir-cook until boils.
8. Reduce heat and simmer for 20 minutes to thicken the sauce.
9. Coat the pork chops with salt and ground black pepper. Serve warm with the prepared sauce.

Nutrition:

- Calories: 346
- Fat: 13.5g
- Saturated Fat: 4g
- Trans Fat: 0g
- Carbohydrates: 27g
- Fiber: 0.5g
- Sodium: 1324mg
- Protein: 27g

7.6 Korean Chili Pork

Prep Time: 5-10 minutes

Cooking Time: 8 minutes

Servings: 4

Ingredients:

- 2 pounds pork, cut into ⅛-inch slices
- 5 minced garlic cloves
- 3 tablespoons minced green onion
- 1 yellow onion, sliced
- ½ cup soy sauce
- ½ cup brown sugar
- 3 tablespoons Korean red chili paste or regular chili paste
- 2 tablespoons sesame seeds
- 3 teaspoons black pepper
- Red pepper flakes to taste

Directions:

1. Take a zip-lock bag, add all the ingredients. Shake well and refrigerate for 6-8 hours to marinate.
2. Take Ninja Foodi Grill, orchestrate it over your kitchen stage, and open the top.
3. Mastermind the barbecue mesh and close the top cover.
4. Click "GRILL" and choose the "MED" grill function. flame broil work. Modify the clock to 8 minutes and afterward press "START/STOP." Ninja Foodi will begin to warm up.
5. Ninja Foodi is preheated and prepared to cook when it begins to signal. After you hear a signal, open the top.
6. Fix finely sliced pork on the barbeque mesh.

7. Cover and cook for 4 minutes. Then open the cover, switch the side of the pork.
8. Cover it and cook for another 4 minutes.
9. Serve warm with chopped lettuce, optional.

Nutrition:
- Calories: 621
- Fat: 31g
- Saturated Fat: 12.5g
- Trans Fat: 0g
- Carbohydrates: 29g
- Fiber: 3g
- Sodium: 1428mg
- Protein: 53g

7.7 Lettuce Cheese Steak

Prep Time: 5-10 minutes
Cooking Time: 16 minutes
Servings: 5-6
Ingredients:
- 4 (8-ounce) skirt steaks
- 6 cups romaine lettuce, chopped
- ¾ cup cherry tomatoes halved
- ¼ cup blue cheese, crumbled
- Ocean salt and Ground Black Pepper
- 2 avocados, peeled and sliced
- 1 cup croutons

- 1 cup blue cheese dressing

Directions:

1. Coat steaks with black pepper and salt.
2. Take Ninja Foodi Grill, mastermind it over your kitchen stage, and open the top. Organize the barbecue mesh and close the top.
3. Click "GRILL" and choose the "HIGH" function. Change the clock to 8 minutes and afterward press "START/STOP." Ninja Foodi will begin pre-warming.
4. Ninja Foodi is preheated and prepared to cook when it begins to blare. After you hear a blare, open the top cover.
5. Fix finely the 2 steaks on the barbeque mesh.
6. Close the top cover and cook for 4 minutes. Presently open the top cover, flip the steaks.
7. Close the top cover and cook for 4 additional minutes. Cook until the food thermometer comes to 165°F. Cook for 3-4 more minutes if needed. Grill the remaining steaks.
8. In a mixing bowl, add the lettuce, tomatoes, blue cheese, and croutons. Combine the ingredients to mix well with each other.
9. Serve the steaks warm with the salad mixture, blue cheese dressing, and avocado slices on top.

Nutrition:

- Calories: 576
- Fat: 21g
- Saturated Fat: 8.5g
- Trans Fat: 0g
- Carbohydrates: 23g
- Fiber: 6.5g
- Sodium: 957mg
- Protein: 53.5g

7.8 Grilled Beef Burgers

Prep Time: 5-10 minutes

Cooking Time: 10 minutes

Servings: 4

Ingredients:

- 4 ounces cream cheese
- 4 slices bacon, cooked and crumbled
- 2 seeded jalapeño peppers, stemmed, and minced
- ½ cup shredded Cheddar cheese
- ½ teaspoon chili powder
- ¼ teaspoon paprika
- ¼ teaspoon ground black pepper
- 2 pounds ground beef
- 4 hamburger buns
- 4 slices pepper Jack cheese
- Optional - Lettuce, sliced tomato, and sliced red onion

Directions:

1. In a mixing bowl, combine the peppers, Cheddar cheese, cream cheese, and bacon until well combined.
2. Prepare the ground beef into 8 patties. Add the cheese mixture onto four of the patties; arrange a second patty on top of each to prepare four burgers. Press gently.
3. In another bowl, combine the chili powder, paprika, and pepper. Sprinkle the mixture onto the sides of the burgers.
4. Take Ninja Foodi Grill, organize it over your kitchen stage, and open the top cover.
5. Organize the flame broil mesh and close the top cover.

6. Press "Flame broil" and select the "HIGH" barbecue work. Change the clock to 4 minutes and afterward press "START/STOP." Ninja Foodi will begin pre-warming.

7. Ninja Foodi is preheated and prepared to cook when it begins to blare. After you hear a blare, open the top. Arrange the burgers over the grill grate.

8. Close the top lid and allow it to cook until the timer reads zero. Cook for 3-4 more minutes, if needed.

9. Cook until the food thermometer reaches 145°F. Serve warm.

10. Serve warm with buns. Add your choice of toppings: pepper Jack cheese, lettuce, tomato, and red onion.

Nutrition:

- Calories: 783
- Fat: 38g
- Saturated Fat: 16g
- Trans Fat: 0g
- Carbohydrates: 25g
- Fiber: 3g
- Sodium: 1259mg
- Protein: 57.5g

8. Meatless Recipes

8.1 Rice & Bean Meal

Prep Time: 5-10 minutes

Cooking Time: 8 minutes

Servings: 4

Ingredients:

- 2 large garlic cloves, minced
- 1 jalapeño pepper, seeded and chopped
- 3 tablespoons olive oil
- 1 small onion, chopped (about ⅔ cup)
- 1 cup long-grain white rice, thoroughly rinsed
- 1 (16-ounce) can pinto beans, depleted and flushed
- ⅓ cup red salsa
- ¼ cup tomato sauce
- ½ cup vegetable stock or broth
- 1 teaspoon Mexican seasoning mix
- 1 teaspoon kosher salt
- 1 tablespoon chopped fresh cilantro (optional)

Directions:

1. Take Ninja Foodi multi-cooker, arrange it over a cooking platform, and open the top lid.
2. In the pot, add the oil; Select "SEAR/SAUTÉ" mode and select "MD: HI" pressure level. Press "STOP/START." After about 4-5 minutes, the oil will start simmering.

3. Add the onions, garlic, jalapeno, and cook (while stirring) until they become softened for 2 minutes.
4. Mix the rice, salsa, tomato sauce, vegetable stock/water, seasoning, pinto beans, and salt.
5. Seal the multi-cooker by locking it with the pressure lid; ensure to keep the pressure release valve locked/sealed.
6. Select "PRESSURE" mode and select the "HI" pressure level. Then, set timer to 6 minutes and press "STOP/START"; it will start the cooking process by building up inside pressure, when the timer goes off, naturally release inside pressure for about 8-10 minutes, then, quick-release pressure by adjusting the pressure valve to the VENT.

Nutrition:

- Calories: 366
- Fat: 11g
- Saturated Fat: 2g
- Trans Fat: 0g
- Carbohydrates: 48.5g
- Fiber: 6.5g
- Sodium: 951mg
- Protein: 11g

8.2 Bacon Potato Soup

Prep Time: 5-10 minutes

Cooking Time: 20 minutes

Servings: 5-6

Ingredients:

- 3 garlic cloves, minced

- 4 pounds Russet potatoes, peeled and chopped
- 4 cups chicken broth
- 5 slices bacon, chopped
- 1 onion, chopped
- 1 cup whole milk
- 1 ½ cups shredded Cheddar cheese
- ½ teaspoon of sea salt
- ½ teaspoon Black pepper (ground)

Directions:

1. Take Ninja Foodi multi-cooker, arrange it over a cooking platform, and open the top lid.
2. In the pot, add the oil, select "SEAR/SAUTÉ" mode and select "MD: HI" pressure level. Press "STOP/START." After about 4-5 minutes, the oil will start simmering.
3. Add the onions, bacon, garlic, and cook (while stirring) until they become softened and translucent for 4-5 minutes.
4. Add the potatoes and chicken broth.
5. Seal the multi-cooker by locking it with the pressure lid, ensure to keep the pressure release valve locked/sealed.
6. Select "PRESSURE" mode and select the "HI" pressure level. Then after, set timer to 10 minutes and press "STOP/START," it will start the cooking process by building up inside pressure.
7. When the timer goes off, quickly release pressure by adjusting the pressure valve to the VENT. After pressure gets released, open the pressure lid.
8. Add the milk and mash the ingredients, season with paper, and salt. Add the cheese on top.
9. Seal the multi-cooker by locking it with the Crisping Lid, ensure to keep the pressure release valve locked/sealed.

10. Select "BROIL" mode and select the "HI" pressure level. Then after, set timer to 5 minutes and press "STOP/START," it will start the cooking process by building up inside pressure.

11. When the timer goes off, quickly release pressure by adjusting the pressure valve to the VENT, after pressure gets released, open the Crisping Lid.

Nutrition:

- Calories: 433
- Fat: 17.5g
- Saturated Fat: 7g
- Trans Fat: 0g
- Carbohydrates: 46g
- Fiber: 7g
- Sodium: 941mg
- Protein: 22.5g

8.3 Pasta Squash Soup

Prep Time: 5-10 minutes
Cooking Time: 30 minutes
Servings: 7-8
Ingredients:

- 1 green apple, cut into small cubes
- 4 slices uncooked bacon, cut into ½-inch pieces
- 12 ounces butternut squash, peeled and cubed
- 1 tablespoon minced oregano
- 2 quarts chicken stock

- Kosher salt and black pepper (ground) to taste
- 1 cup orzo

Directions:

1. Take Ninja Foodi multi-cooker, arrange it over a cooking platform, and open the top lid.
2. Select "SEAR/SAUTÉ" mode and select "MD: HI" pressure level. Press "STOP/START".
3. Add the bacon and cook (while stirring) until it becomes crisp for 4-5 minutes, and fat is rendered. Set aside the bacon and place over paper towels.
4. Keep the fat in the pot, add the butternut squash, apple, salt, and pepper, stir cook for about 5 minutes. Mix in the stock, oregano, and bacon.
5. Set "SEAR/SAUTÉ" mode to "HI" and boil the mixture for 10 minutes. Mix in the pasta and stir cook for about 8 minutes.

Nutrition:

- Calories: 253
- Fat: 6.5g
- Saturated Fat: 2g
- Trans Fat: 0g
- Carbohydrates: 32g
- Fiber: 3.5g
- Sodium: 533mg
- Protein: 12g

8.4 Mustard Green Veggies

Prep Time: 5-10 minutes

Cooking Time: 30-40 minutes

Servings: 7-8

Ingredients:

Vinaigrette:

- 2 tablespoon Dijon mustard
- 1/2 cup red wine vinegar
- 2 tablespoon honey
- 1 teaspoon salt
- 1/4 teaspoon black pepper
- 1/2 cup avocado oil
- 1/2 cup olive oil

Veggies:

- 4 zucchinis, halved
- 4 sweet onions, quartered
- 4 red peppers, seeded and halved
- 2 bunches green onions, trimmed
- 4 yellow squash, cut in half

Directions:

1. In a little bowl, whisk the vinegar, mustard, nectar, pepper, and salt. Include the oils and join them to make a smooth blend.
2. Take Ninja Foodi Grill, organize it over your kitchen stage, and open the top.
3. Organize the flame broil mesh and close the top cover.
4. Press "Flame broil" and select the "Drug" barbecue work. Modify the clock to 10 minutes and afterward press "START/STOP." Ninja Foodi will begin pre-warming.

5. Ninja Foodi is preheated and prepared to cook when it begins to blare. After you hear a blare, open the top.
6. Arrange the onion quarters over the grill grate.
7. Close the top lid and cook for 5 minutes. Now open the top lid, flip the onions.
8. Close the top lid and cook for 5 more minutes.
9. Grill the other vegetables in the same manner with 7 minutes per side for the zucchini, peppers, and squash, and 1 minute per side for the green onions.
10. Serve the grilled veggies with the vinaigrette on top.

Nutrition:
- Calories: 326
- Fat: 4.5g
- Saturated Fat: 0.5g
- Trans Fat: 0g
- Carbohydrates: 35.5g
- Fiber: 2g
- Sodium: 524mg
- Protein: 8g

8.5 Creamy Corn Potatoes

Prep Time: 5-10 minutes

Cooking Time: 30-40 minutes

Servings: 4

Ingredients:
- 1 1/2-pound red potatoes, quartered and boiled
- 3 tablespoons olive oil

- 1 tablespoon cilantro, minced
- 2 sweet corn ears, without husks
- 1/4 teaspoon cayenne pepper
- 2 poblano peppers
- 1/2 cup milk
- 1 teaspoon ground cumin
- 1 tablespoon lime juice
- 1 jalapeno pepper, seeded and minced
- 1/2 cup sour cream
- 1 ½ teaspoons garlic salt

Directions:

1. Drain the potatoes and rub them with oil.
2. Take Ninja Foodi Grill, orchestrate it over your kitchen stage, and open the top cover.
3. Orchestrate the flame broil mesh and close the top.
4. Press "Barbecue" and select the "MED" flame broil work. Change the clock to 10 minutes and afterward press "START/STOP." Ninja Foodi will begin pre-warming.
5. Ninja Foodi is preheated and prepared to cook when it begins to blare. After you hear a blare, open the top cover.
6. Arrange the poblano peppers over the grill grate.
7. Close the top lid and cook for 5 minutes. Now open the top lid, flip the peppers.
8. Close the top lid and cook for 5 more minutes.
9. Grill the other vegetables in the same manner with 7 minutes per side for the potatoes and corn.
10. Whisk the remaining ingredients in another bowl.

11. Peel the grilled pepper and chop them. Divide corn ears into smaller pieces and cut the potatoes as well.
12. Serve the grilled veggies with the vinaigrette on top.

Nutrition:
- Calories: 322
- Fat: 4.5g
- Saturated Fat: 1g
- Trans Fat: 0g
- Carbohydrates: 51.5g
- Fiber: 3g
- Sodium: 600mg
- Protein: 5g

8.6 Eggplant Pasta Delight

Prep Time: 5-10 minutes

Cooking Time: 10 minutes

Servings: 4

Ingredients:
- 1 tablespoon capers, drained and rinsed, minced
- 1 tablespoon minced garlic
- 8-ounces dried whole wheat ziti
- 1 small red onion, chopped
- 1-pound eggplant, stemmed and diced
- 1 (28-ounce) can diced tomatoes about 3 ½ cups
- 1 ¼ cups vegetable broth

- 2 tablespoons canned tomato paste
- 2 medium yellow bell peppers, stemmed, cored and chopped
- 2 tablespoons olive oil
- 2 teaspoons dried rosemary
- 1 teaspoon dried thyme
- 1/2 teaspoon ground black pepper

Directions:

1. Take Ninja Foodi multi-cooker, arrange it over a cooking platform, and open the top lid.
2. In the pot, add the oil, select "SEAR/SAUTÉ" mode and select "MD: HI" pressure level. Press "STOP/START." After about 4-5 minutes, the oil will start simmering.
3. Add the onions, capers, garlic, and cook (while stirring) until they become softened and translucent for 2 minutes.
4. Add the eggplant and bell peppers, stir-cook for 1 minute. Mix in the pasta, tomatoes, broth, tomato paste, rosemary, thyme, and pepper.
5. Seal the multi-cooker by locking it with the pressure lid, ensure to keep the pressure release valve locked/sealed.
6. Select "PRESSURE" mode and select the "HI" pressure level. Then after, set timer to 8 minutes and press "STOP/START," it will start the cooking process by building up inside pressure.
7. When the timer goes off, quickly release pressure by adjusting the pressure valve to the VENT. After pressure gets released, open the pressure lid.

Nutrition:

- Calories: 278
- Fat: 8g
- Saturated Fat: 1g
- Trans Fat: 0g

- Carbohydrates: 44g
- Fiber: 4g
- Sodium: 754mg
- Protein: 8.5g

8.7 Healthy Broccoli Salad

Prep Time: 5-10 minutes
Cooking Time: 15 minutes
Servings: 4
Ingredients:

- 1 red onion; chopped
- 1/2 cup almonds; sliced
- 2 broccoli heads; florets chopped
- 2 carrots; shredded
- 1 tablespoon olive oil
- 3 tablespoons apple cider vinegar
- 1/2 cup cranberries; dried
- Black pepper (finely ground) and salt to the taste

Directions:

1. Take Ninja Foodi multi-cooker, arrange it over a cooking platform, and open the top lid.
2. In the pot, add the ingredients one by one. Stir gently.
3. Seal the multi-cooker by locking it with the pressure lid; ensure to keep the pressure release valve locked/sealed.

4. Select "PRESSURE" mode and select the "HI" pressure level. Then, set timer to 15 minutes and press "STOP/START"; it will start the cooking process by building up inside pressure.

5. When the timer goes off, quickly release pressure by adjusting the pressure valve to the VENT. After pressure gets released, open the pressure lid.

Nutrition:

- Calories: 165
- Fat: 5g
- Saturated Fat: 1g
- Trans Fat: 0g
- Carbohydrates: 21.5g
- Fiber: 5g
- Sodium: 87mg
- Protein: 3g

8.8 Veggie Rice Soup

Prep Time: 5-10 minutes

Cooking Time: 30 minutes

Servings: 5-6

Ingredients:

- 1 onion, chopped
- 3 garlic cloves, minced
- 5 medium carrots, chopped
- 5 celery stalks, chopped
- 1 cup wild rice

- 1 teaspoon kosher salt
- 1 teaspoon poultry seasoning
- ½ teaspoon dried thyme
- 8 ounces mushrooms, sliced
- 6 cups vegetable broth

Directions:

1. Take Ninja Foodi multi-cooker, arrange it over a cooking platform, and open the top lid.
2. In the pot, add the ingredients one by one. Stir gently.
3. Seal the multi-cooker by locking it with the pressure lid; ensure to keep the pressure release valve locked/sealed.
4. Select "PRESSURE" mode and select the "HI" pressure level. Then, set timer to 30 minutes and press "STOP/START"; it will start the cooking process by building up inside pressure.
5. When the timer goes off, quickly release pressure by adjusting the pressure valve to the VENT. After pressure gets released, open the pressure lid.

Nutrition:

- Calories: 198
- Fat: 3.5g
- Saturated Fat: 0.5g
- Trans Fat: 0g
- Carbohydrates: 26.5g
- Fiber: 3.5g
- Sodium: 654mg
- Protein: 11g

9. Vegetarian

9.1 Tomato Salsa

Prep Time: 5-10 minutes
Cooking Time: 10 minutes
Servings: 4
Ingredients:

- 1 red onion, peeled, cut in quarters
- 1 jalapeño pepper, cut in half, seeds removed
- 5 Roma tomatoes, cut in half lengthwise
- 1 tablespoon kosher salt
- 2 teaspoons ground black pepper
- 2 tablespoons canola oil
- 1 bunch cilantro, stems trimmed
- Juice and zest of 3 limes
- 3 cloves garlic, peeled
- 2 tablespoons ground cumin

Directions:

1. In a blending bowl, join the onion, tomatoes, jalapeño pepper, salt, dark pepper, and canola oil.
2. Take Ninja Foodi Grill, mastermind it over your kitchen stage, and open the top. Mastermind the barbecue mesh and close the top cover.
3. Press "Barbecue" and select the "Maximum" flame broil work. Change the clock to 10 minutes and afterward press "START/STOP." Ninja Foodi will begin preheating.

4. Ninja Foodi is preheated and prepared to cook when it begins to blare. After you hear a signal, open the top cover.
5. Arrange the vegetables over the grill grate.
6. Close the top lid and cook for 5 minutes. Now open the top lid, flip the vegetables.
7. Close the top lid and cook for five more minutes.
8. Blend the mixture in a blender and serve as needed.

Nutrition:
- Calories: 169
- Fat: 9g
- Saturated Fat: 2g
- Trans Fat: 0g
- Carbohydrates: 12g
- Fiber: 3g
- Sodium: 321mg
- Protein: 2.5g

9.2 Mushroom Tomato Roast

Prep Time: 10 minutes

Cooking Time: 15 minutes

Servings: 4

Ingredients:
- 2 cups cherry tomatoes
- 2 cups cremini, button, or other small mushrooms
- 1/4 cup of vinegar (Sherry) or 1/4 cup of red wine
- 2 garlic cloves, finely chopped

- 1/2 cup extra-virgin olive oil
- 3 tablespoons chopped thyme
- Pinch of crushed red pepper flakes
- 1 teaspoon kosher salt
- 1/2 teaspoon black pepper
- 6 scallions, cut crosswise into 2-inch pieces

Directions:

1. Take a zip-lock bag, add black pepper, salt, red pepper flakes, thyme, vinegar, oil, and garlic. Add mushrooms, tomatoes, and scallions.
2. Shake well and refrigerate for 30-40 minutes to marinate.
3. Take Ninja Foodi Grill, orchestrate it over your kitchen stage, and open the top.
4. Press "Prepare" and alter the temperature to 400°F. Modify the clock to 12 minutes and afterward press "START/STOP." Ninja Foodi will begin preheating.
5. Ninja Foodi is preheated and prepared to cook when it begins to blare. After you hear a blare, open the top.
6. Arrange the mushroom mixture directly inside the pot.
7. Close the top lid and allow it to cook until the timer reads zero.
8. Serve warm.

Nutrition:

- Calories: 253
- Fat: 24g   Saturated Fat: 4g
- Trans Fat: 0g
- Carbohydrates: 7g
- Fiber: 2g
- Sodium: 546mg
- Protein: 1g

9.3 Cheddar Cauliflower Meal

Prep Time: 5-10 minutes

Cooking Time: 15 minutes

Servings: 2

Ingredients:

- ½ teaspoon garlic powder
- ½ teaspoon paprika
- Ocean salt and ground dark pepper to taste
- 1 head cauliflower, stemmed and leaves removed
- 1 cup Cheddar cheese, shredded
- Ranch dressing, for garnish
- ¼ cup canola oil or vegetable oil
- 2 tablespoons chopped chives
- 4 slices bacon, cooked and crumbled

Directions:

1. Cut the cauliflower into 2-inch pieces.
2. In a blending bowl, include the oil, garlic powder, and paprika. Season with salt and ground dark pepper; join well. Coat the florets with the blend.
3. Take Ninja Foodi Grill, mastermind it over your kitchen stage, and open the top cover.
4. Mastermind the flame broil mesh and close the top cover.
5. Press "Flame broil" and select the "Maximum" barbecue work. Change the clock to 15 minutes and afterward press "START/STOP." Ninja Foodi will begin preheating.
6. Ninja Foodi is preheated and prepared to cook when it begins to signal. After you hear a blare, open the top.
7. Organize the pieces over the flame broil grind.

8. Close the top lid and cook for 10 minutes. Now open the top lid, flip the pieces and top with the cheese.

9. Close the top lid and cook for 5 more minutes. Serve warm with the chives and ranch dressing on top.

Nutrition:
- Calories: 534
- Fat: 34g
- Saturated Fat: 13g
- Trans Fat: 0g
- Carbohydrates: 14.5g
- Fiber: 4g
- Sodium: 1359mg
- Protein: 31g

9.4 Buttery Spinach Meal

Prep Time: 10 minutes
Cooking Time: 15 minutes
Servings: 4
Ingredients:
- 2/3 cup Kalamata olives, halved and pitted
- 1 and ½ cups feta cheese, grated
- 4 tablespoons butter
- 2 pounds spinach, chopped and boiled
- Pepper and salt to taste
- 4 teaspoons lemon zest, grated

Directions:

1. Take a mixing bowl and add spinach, butter, salt, pepper and mix well
2. Pre-heat Ninja Foodi by pressing the "AIR CRISP" option and setting it to "340 Degrees F" and timer to 15 minutes
3. Let it pre-heat until you hear a beep
4. Arrange a reversible trivet in the Grill Pan, arrange spinach mixture in a basket and place basket in the trivet
5. Let them roast until the timer runs out
6. Serve and enjoy!

Nutrition:

- Calories: 250
- Fat: 18 g
- Saturated Fat: 6 g
- Carbohydrates: 8 g
- Fiber: 3 g
- Sodium: 309 mg
- Protein: 10 g

9.5 Mustard Green Veggie Meal

Prep Time: 10 minutes

Cooking Time: 30-40 minutes

Servings: 4

Ingredients:

Vinaigrette:

- 2 tablespoons Dijon mustard
- 1 teaspoon salt
- ¼ teaspoon black pepper

- ½ cup avocado oil
- ½ olive oil
- ½ cup red wine vinegar
- 2 tablespoons honey

Veggies:

- 4 sweet onions, quartered
- 4 yellow squash, cut in half
- 4 red peppers, seeded and halved
- 4 zucchinis, halved
- 2 bunches green onions, trimmed

Directions:

1. Take a small bowl and whisk mustard, pepper, honey, vinegar, and salt
2. Add oil to make a smooth mixture
3. Mastermind the flame broil mesh and close the top cover
4. Pre-heat Ninja Foodi by pressing the "GRILL" option and setting it to "MED" and timer to 10 minutes
5. Let it pre-heat until you hear a beep
6. Arrange the onion quarters over the grill grate, lock lid and cook for 5 minutes
7. Flip the peppers and cook for 5 minutes more
8. Grill the other vegetables in the same manner with 7 minutes each side for zucchini, pepper, and squash and 1 minute for onion
9. Prepare the vinaigrette by mixing all the ingredients under vinaigrette in a bowl
10. Serve the grilled veggies with vinaigrette on top
11. Enjoy!

Nutrition:

- Calories: 326
- Fat: 4.5 g
- Saturated Fat: 1 g
- Carbohydrates: 35 g
- Fiber: 4 g
- Sodium: 543 mg
- Protein: 8 g

9.6 Broccoli and Arugula Salad

Prep Time: 10 minutes
Cooking Time: 12 minutes
Servings: 4
Ingredients:

- 2 heads broccoli, trimmed into florets
- 4 cups arugula, torn
- 2 tablespoons parmesan cheese, grated
- 1 tablespoon lemon juice
- 1 teaspoon honey
- 1 teaspoon Dijon mustard
- 1 garlic clove, minced
- ½ red onion, sliced
- 1 tablespoon canola oil
- 2 tablespoons extra-virgin olive oil
- Red pepper flakes
- ¼ teaspoon of sea salt

- Black pepper, freshly grounded

Directions:

1. Supplement the flame broil mesh and close the hood
2. Pre-heat Ninja Foodi by pressing the "GRILL" option at and setting it to "MAX" and timer to 12 minutes
3. Take a large bowl and combine the broccoli, sliced onions, canola oil
4. Toss until coated
5. Once it pre-heat until you hear a beep
6. Arrange the vegetables over the grill grate, lock lid and cook for 8 to 12 minutes
7. Take a medium bowl and whisk together lemon juice, mustard, olive oil, honey, garlic, red pepper flakes, salt, and pepper
8. Once cooked, combine the roasted vegetables and arugula in a large serving bowl
9. Drizzle with the vinaigrette to taste and sprinkle with parmesan cheese
10. Serve and enjoy!

Nutrition:

- Calories: 168
- Fat: 12 g
- Saturated Fat: 3 g
- Carbohydrates: 13 g
- Fiber: 1 g
- Sodium: 392 mg
- Protein: 6 g

9.7 Mustard Green Veggies

Prep Time: 5-10 minutes

Cooking Time: 30-40 minutes

Servings: 7-8

Ingredients:

Vinaigrette:

- 2 tablespoon Dijon mustard
- 1/2 cup red wine vinegar
- 2 tablespoon honey
- 1 teaspoon salt
- 1/4 teaspoon black pepper
- 1/2 cup avocado oil
- 1/2 cup olive oil

Veggies:

- 4 zucchinis, halved
- 4 sweet onions, quartered
- 4 red peppers, seeded and halved
- 2 bunches green onions, trimmed
- 4 yellow squash, cut in half

Directions:

1. In a little bowl, whisk the vinegar, mustard, nectar, pepper, and salt. Include the oils and consolidate them to make a smooth blend.
2. Take Ninja Foodi Grill, organize it over your kitchen stage, and open the top.
3. Organize the barbecue mesh and close the top cover.

4. Press "Flame broil" and select the "Drug" barbecue work. Alter the clock to 10 minutes and afterward press "START/STOP." Ninja Foodi will begin pre-warming.
5. Ninja Foodi is preheated and prepared to cook when it begins to blare. After you hear a signal, open the top.
6. Arrange the onion quarters over the grill grate.
7. Close the top lid and cook for 5 minutes. Now open the top lid, flip the onions.
8. Close the top lid and cook for 5 more minutes.
9. Grill the other vegetables in the same manner with 7 minutes per side for the zucchini, peppers, and squash. And 1 minute per side for the green onions.
10. Serve the grilled veggies with the vinaigrette on top.

Nutrition:

- Calories: 326
- Fat: 4.5g
- Saturated Fat: 0.5g
- Trans Fat: 0g
- Carbohydrates: 35.5g
- Fiber: 2g
- Sodium: 524mg
- Protein: 8g

9.8 Creamy Corn Potatoes

Prep Time: 5-10 minutes

Cooking Time: 30-40 minutes

Servings: 4

Ingredients:

- 1 1/2-pound red potatoes, quartered and boiled
- 3 tablespoons olive oil
- 1 tablespoon cilantro, minced
- 2 sweet corn ears, without husks
- 1/4 teaspoon cayenne pepper
- 2 poblano peppers
- 1/2 cup milk
- 1 teaspoon ground cumin
- 1 tablespoon lime juice
- 1 jalapeno pepper, seeded and minced
- 1/2 cup sour cream
- 1 ½ teaspoons garlic salt

Directions:

1. Drain the potatoes and rub them with oil.
2. Take Ninja Foodi Grill, mastermind it over your kitchen stage, and open the top cover.
3. Mastermind the flame broil mesh and close the top cover.
4. Press "Flame broil" and select the "Drug" barbecue work. Modify the clock to 10 minutes and afterward press "START/STOP." Ninja Foodi will begin pre-warming.

5. Ninja Foodi is preheated and prepared to cook when it begins to blare. After you hear a signal, open the top cover.
6. Arrange the poblano peppers over the grill grate.
7. Close the top lid and cook for 5 minutes. Now open the top lid, flip the peppers.
8. Close the top lid and cook for 5 more minutes.
9. Grill the other vegetables in the same manner with 7 minutes per side for the potatoes and corn.
10. Whisk the remaining ingredients in another bowl.
11. Peel the grilled pepper and chop them. Divide corn ears into smaller pieces and cut the potatoes as well.
12. Serve the grilled veggies with the vinaigrette on top.

Nutrition:

- Calories: 322   Fat: 4.5g
- Saturated Fat: 1g
- Trans Fat: 0g   Carbohydrates: 51.5g
- Fiber: 3g
- Sodium: 600mg
- Protein: 5g

9.9 Classic Bruschetta

Prep Time: 5-10 minutes
Cooking Time: 4 minutes
Servings: 8
Ingredients:
Tomato mixture:

- 1-pound plum tomatoes, seeded and chopped

- 1 cup chopped celery or fennel bulb
- 1/4 cup minced basil
- 3 tablespoons balsamic vinegar
- 3 tablespoons olive oil
- 3 tablespoons Dijon mustard
- 1/2 teaspoon salt
- 2 garlic cloves, minced
- Mayonnaise Spread:
- 3/4 teaspoon dried oregano
- 1/4 cup Dijon mustard
- 1/2 cup mayonnaise
- 1 garlic clove, minced
- 1 tablespoon finely chopped green onion
- 1 loaf (1 pound) French bread, cut into 1/2-inch slices

Directions:

1. In a mixing bowl, add the tomato mixture ingredients. Combine the ingredients to mix well with each other. Cover and refrigerate for 30-60 minutes.
2. In another bowl, combine the mayonnaise, mustard, onion, garlic, and oregano.
3. Take Ninja Foodi Grill, mastermind it over your kitchen stage, and open the top cover. Orchestrate the flame broil mesh and close the top.
4. Press "Flame broil" and select the "Drug" barbecue work. Modify the clock to 4 minutes and afterward press "START/STOP." Ninja Foodi will begin preheating.
5. Ninja Foodi is preheated and prepared to cook when it begins to signal. After you hear a signal, open the top cover.

6. Arrange the bread slices over the grill grate. Close the top lid and cook for 2 minutes. Now open the top lid, flip the slices and spread with the mayo mixture. Close the top lid and cook for 2 more minutes. Serve warm with the tomato mixture on top.

Nutrition:

- Calories: 241
- Fat: 15.5g
- Saturated Fat: 3g
- Trans Fat: 0g
- Carbohydrates: 24.5g
- Fiber: 4g
- Sodium: 526mg
- Protein: 8g

10. Dessert

10.1 Cashew Cream

Prep Time: 18 minutes

Cooking Time: 10 minutes

Servings: 10

Ingredients:

- 3 cups cashew
- 2 cups chicken stock
- 1 teaspoon salt
- 1 tablespoon butter
- 2 tablespoons ricotta cheese

Directions:

1. Combine the cashews with the chicken stock in the Multicooker.
2. Add salt and close the Multicooker lid. Cook the dish on the" Pressure" mode for 10 minutes.
3. Remove the cashews from the Multicooker and drain the nuts from the water. Transfer the cashews to a blender and add the ricotta cheese and butter.
4. Blend the mixture until it is smooth. When you get the texture you want, remove it from a blender. Serve it immediately or keep the cashew butter in the refrigerator.

Nutrition:

- calories 252
- fat 20.6g   carbs 13.8g
- protein 6.8g

10.2 Blackberry Cake

Prep Time: 35 minutes

Cooking Time: 25 minutes

Servings: 4

Ingredients:

- 4 tablespoons butter
- 3 tablespoon Erythritol
- 2 eggs, whisked
- ½ teaspoon vanilla extract
- 1 oz blackberries
- 1 cup almond flour
- ½ teaspoon baking powder

Directions:

1. Combine together all the liquid ingredients.
2. Then add baking powder, almond flour, and Erythritol.
3. Stir the mixture until smooth.
4. Add blackberries and stir the batter gently with the help of the spoon.
5. Take the non-sticky springform pan and transfer the batter inside.
6. Place the springform pan in the pot and lower the air fryer lid.
7. Cook the cake for 20 minutes at 365 F.
8. When the time is over – check the doneness of the cake with the help of the toothpick and cook for 5 minutes more if needed.
9. Chill it little and serve!

Nutrition:

- Calories: 173
- Fat: 16.7g

- Carbohydrates: 2.2g
- Protein: 4.2g

10.3 The Original Pot-De-Crème

Prep Time: 30 minutes

Cooking Time: 12 minutes

Servings: 4

Ingredients:

- 6 egg yolks
- 2 cups heavy whip cream
- 1/3 cup cocoa powder
- 1 tablespoon pure vanilla extract
- ½ teaspoon liquid stevia
- Whipped coconut cream as needed for garnish
- Shaved dark chocolate, for garnish

Directions:

1. Take a medium bowl and whisk in yolks, heavy cream, cocoa powder, vanilla and stevia
2. Pour the mixture into 1 and ½ quart baking dish and place the dish in your multi-cooker insert
3. Add enough water to reach about halfway up the sides of baking dish
4. Lock lid and cook on HIGH pressure for 12 minutes
5. Quick release pressure once the cycle is complete
6. Remove baking dish from insert and let it cool
7. Chill the dessert in refrigerator and serve with garnish of whipped coconut cream and shaved dark chocolate

8. Enjoy!

Nutrition:
- Calories: 275
- Fat: 18g
- Carbohydrates: 3g
- Protein: 5g

10.4 Cinnamon Bun

Prep Time: 25 minutes

Cooking Time: 15 minutes

Servings: 8

Ingredients:
- 1 cup almond flour
- ½ teaspoon baking powder
- 3 tablespoon Erythritol
- 2 tablespoon ground cinnamon
- ½ teaspoon vanilla extract
- 1 tablespoon butter
- 1 egg, whisked
- ¾ teaspoon salt
- ¼ cup almond milk

Directions:
1. Mix up together the almond flour, baking powder, vanilla extract, egg, salt, and almond milk.
2. Knead the soft and non-sticky dough.
3. Roll up the dough with the help of the rolling pin

4. Sprinkle dough with the butter, cinnamon, and Erythritol.
5. Roll the dough into the log.
6. Cut the roll into 7 pieces.
7. Spray multi-cooker basket with the cooking spray.
8. Place the cinnamon buns in the basket and close the lid.
9. Set the Bake mode and cook the buns for 15 minutes at 355F
10. Check if the buns are cooked with the help of the toothpick.
11. Chill the buns well and serve!

Nutrition:
- Calories: 292
- Fat: 26g
- Carbohydrates: 8g
- Protein: 5g

10.5 Lemon Mousse

Prep Time: 15 minutes

Cooking time: 12 minutes

Servings: 2

Ingredients:
- 4 ounces cream cheese softened
- ½ cup heavy cream
- 1/8 cup fresh lemon juice
- ½ teaspoon lemon liquid stevia
- 2 pinches salt

Directions:

1. Take a bowl and mix cream cheese, heavy cream, lemon juice, salt, and stevia.
2. Pour this mixture into the ramekins and transfer the ramekins in the pot of Ninja Foodi.
3. Select "Bake/Roast" and bake for 12 minutes at 350 degrees F.
4. Pour into the serving glasses and refrigerate for at least 3 hours.

Nutrition:

- Calories 305,
- Total Fat 31 g,
- Saturated Fat 19.5 g,
- Cholesterol 103 mg,
- Sodium 299 mg,
- Total Carbs 2.7 g,
- Fiber 0.1 g,
- Sugar 0.5 g,
- Protein 5 g

10.6 Chocolate Cheesecake

Prep Time: 15 minutes
Cooking time: 15 minutes
Servings: 6
Ingredients:

- 2 cups cream cheese, softened
- 2 eggs
- 2 tablespoons cocoa powder
- 1 teaspoon pure vanilla extract

- ½ cup Swerve

Directions:

1. Add eggs, cocoa powder, vanilla extract, swerve, cream cheese in an immersion blender and blend until smooth.
2. Pour the mixture evenly into mason jars.
3. Put the mason jars in the insert of Ninja Foodi and close the lid.
4. Select "Bake/Roast" and bake for 15 minutes at 360 degrees F.
5. Refrigerate for at least 2 hours.

Nutrition:

- Calories 244,
- Total Fat 24.8 g,
- Saturated Fat 15.6 g,
- Cholesterol 32 mg,
- Sodium 204 mg,
- Total Carbs 2.1 g,
- Fiber 0.1 g,
- Sugar 0.4 g,
- Protein 4 g

10.7 Vanilla Yogurt

Prep Time: 15 minutes

Cooking time: 3 hours

Servings: 2

Ingredients:

- ½ cup full-fat milk
- ¼ cup yogurt starter

- 1 cup heavy cream
- ½ tablespoon pure vanilla extract
- 2 scoops stevia

Directions:

1. Add milk, heavy cream, vanilla extract, and stevia in Ninja Foodi.
2. Let yogurt sit and press "slow cooker" and set the timer to 4 hours on "low."
3. Add yogurt starter in 1 cup of milk.
4. Return this mixture to the pot.
5. Close the lid and wrap the Ninja Foodi in small towels.
6. Let yogurt sit for about 9 hours.
7. Dish out, refrigerate and then serve.

Nutrition:

- Calories 292,
- Total Fat 26.2 g,
- Saturated Fat 16.3 g,
- Cholesterol 100 mg,
- Sodium 86 mg,
- Total Carbs 8.2 g,
- Fiber 0 g,
- Sugar 6.6 g,
- Protein 5.2 g

10.8 Coffee Custard

Prep Time: 15 minutes

Cooking time: 10 minutes

Servings: 4

Ingredients:

- 4 ounces mascarpone cream cheese
- 1 teaspoon espresso powder
- ¼ cup unsalted butter
- 4 large organic eggs, whites and yolks separated
- 1 tablespoon water
- ¼ teaspoon cream of tartar
- ½ teaspoon liquid stevia
- ¼ teaspoon monk fruit extract drops

Directions:

1. Select sauté and "Lo: Md" on Ninja Foodi and add butter and cream cheese, sauté for 3 minutes and mix in espresso powder, egg yolks, and water.
2. Select "low" and cook for 4 minutes.
3. Take a bowl and whisk together egg whites, fruit drops, stevia, and cream of tartar.
4. Pour in the egg white mixture in the mixture present in Ninja Foodi and cook for 3 minutes.
5. Pour it into serving glasses and refrigerate it for 3 hours.

Nutrition:

- Calories 292,
- Total Fat 26.2 g,

- Saturated Fat 16.3 g,
- Cholesterol 100 mg,
- Sodium 86 mg,
- Total Carbs 8.2 g,
- Fiber 0 g,
- Sugar 6.6 g,
- Protein 5.2 g

10.9 Chocolate Fudge

Prep Time: 15 minutes

Cooking time: 6 hours

Servings: 24

Ingredients:

- ½ teaspoon organic vanilla extract
- 1 cup heavy whipping cream
- 2 ounces butter softened
- 2 ounces 70% dark chocolate, finely chopped

Directions:

1. Select sauté and "Md: Hi" on Ninja Foodi and add vanilla and heavy cream, sauté for 5 minutes at "low."
2. Sauté for 10 minutes and add butter and chocolate.
3. Sauté for 2 minutes and pour this mixture into a serving dish.
4. Refrigerate it for some hours and serve.

Nutrition:

- Calories 292,
- Total Fat 26.2 g,

- Saturated Fat 16.3 g,
- Cholesterol 100 mg,
- Sodium 86 mg,
- Total Carbs 8.2 g,
- Fiber 0 g,
- Sugar 6.6 g,
- Protein 5.2 g

10.10 Lime Cheesecake

Prep Time: 15 minutes
Cooking time: 30 minutes
Servings: 6

Ingredients:

- ¼ cup plus 1 teaspoon Erythritol
- 8 ounces cream cheese, softened
- 1/3 cup Ricotta cheese
- 1 teaspoon fresh lime zest, grated
- 2 tablespoons fresh lime juice
- ½ teaspoon organic vanilla extract
- 2 organic eggs
- 2 tablespoons sour cream

Directions:

1. In a bowl, add ¼ cup of Erythritol and remaining ingredients except eggs and sour cream and with a hand mixer beat on high speed until smooth.
2. Add the eggs and beat on low speed until well combined.

3. Transfer the mixture into a 6-inch greased springform pan evenly.
4. With a piece of foil, cover the pan.
5. In the pot of Ninja Foodi, place 2 cups of water.
6. Arrange a "Reversible Rack" in the pot of Ninja Foodi.
7. Place the springform pan over the "Reversible Rack".
8. Close the Ninja Foodi with pressure lid and place the pressure valve to "Seal" position.
9. Select "Pressure" and set to "High" for 30 minutes.
10. Press "Start/Stop" to begin cooking.
11. Switch the valve to "Vent" and do a "Natural" release.
12. Place the pan onto a wire rack to cool slightly.
13. Meanwhile, in a small bowl, add the sour cream and remaining Truvia and beat until well combined.
14. Spread the cream mixture on the warm cake evenly.
15. Refrigerate for about 6-8 hours before serving.

Nutrition:

- Calories: 182,
- Fats: 16.6g,
- Net Carbs: 2.1g,
- Carbs: 2.1g,
- Fiber: 0g,
- Sugar: 0.3g,
- Proteins: 6.4g,
- Sodium: 152mg

10.11 Lemon Cheesecake

Prep Time: 15 minutes
Cooking time: 4 hours
Servings: 12

Ingredients:

For Crust:

- 1½ cups almond flour
- 4 tablespoons butter, melted
- 3 tablespoons sugar-free peanut butter
- 3 tablespoons Erythritol
- 1 large organic egg, beaten

For Filling:

- 1 cup ricotta cheese
- 24 ounces cream cheese, softened
- 1½ cups Erythritol
- 2 teaspoons liquid stevia
- 1/3 cup heavy cream
- 2 large organic eggs
- 3 large organic egg yolks
- 1 tablespoon fresh lemon juice
- 1 tablespoon organic vanilla extract

Directions:

1. Grease the pot of Ninja Foodi.
2. For crust: in a bowl, add all the ingredients and mix until well combined.

3. In the pot of prepared of Ninja Foodi, place the crust mixture and press to smooth the top surface.
4. With a fork, prick the crust at many places.
5. For filling: in a food processor, add the ricotta cheese and pulse until smooth.
6. In a large bowl, add the ricotta, cream cheese, Erythritol and stevia and with an electric mixer, beat over medium speed until smooth.
7. In another bowl, add the heavy cream, eggs, egg yolks, lemon juice and vanilla extract and beat until well combined.
8. Add the egg mixture into cream cheese mixture and beat over medium speed until just combined.
9. Place the filling mixture over crust evenly.
10. Close the Ninja Foodi with crisping lid and select "Slow Cooker".
11. Set on "Low" for 3-4 hours.
12. Press "Start/Stop" to begin cooking.
13. Place the pan onto a wire racks to cool.
14. Refrigerate to chill for at least 6-8 hours before serving.

Nutrition:
- Calories: 410,
- Fats: 37.9g,
- Net Carbs: 5.1g,
- Carbs: 6.9g,
- Fiber: 1.8g,
- Sugar: 1.3g,
- Proteins: 13g,
- Sodium: 260mg

10.12 Strawberry Crumble

Prep Time: 15 minutes
Cooking time: 2 hours
Servings: 5

Ingredients:

- 1 cup almond flour
- 2 tablespoons butter, melted
- 8-10 drops liquid stevia
- 3-4 cups fresh strawberries, hulled and sliced
- 1 tablespoon butter, chopped

Directions:

1. Lightly, grease the pot of Ninja Foodi.
2. In a bowl, add the flour, melted butter and stevia and mix until a crumbly mixture form.
3. In the pot of the prepared Ninja Foodi, place the strawberry slices and dot with chopped butter.
4. Spread the flour mixture on top evenly
5. Close the Ninja Foodi with crisping lid and select "Slow Cooker".
6. Set on "Low" for 2 hours.
7. Press "Start/Stop" to begin cooking.
8. Place the pan onto a wire racks to cool slightly.

Nutrition:

- Calories: 233g
- Fats: 19.2g
- Net Carbs: 6.6g
- Carbs: 10.7g
- Fiber: 4.1g

- Sugar: 5g
- Proteins: 0.7g
- Sodium: 50mg

10.13 Peanut Butter Cups

Prep Time: 15 minutes
Cooking time: 30 minutes
Servings: 3
Ingredients:

- 1 cup butter
- ¼ cup heavy cream
- 2 ounces unsweetened chocolate
- ¼ cup peanut butter, separated
- 4 packets stevia

Directions:

1. Melt the peanut butter and butter in a bowl and stir well with unsweetened chocolate, stevia, and cream.
2. Mix well and pour the mixture in a baking mold.
3. Put the baking mold in the Ninja Foodi and press "Bake/Roast."
4. Set the timer for 30 minutes at 360 degrees F and dish out to serve.

Nutrition:

- Calories 479
- Total Fat 51.5 g   Saturated Fat 29.7 g
- Cholesterol 106 mg
- Sodium 69 mg
- Total Carbs 7.7 g

- Fiber 2.7 g
- Sugar 1.4 g
- Protein 5.2 g

10.14 Chocolate Brownies

Prep Time: 15 minutes
Cooking time: 32 minutes
Servings: 4
Ingredients:

- 3 eggs
- ½ cup butter
- ½ cup sugar-free chocolate chips
- 2 scoops stevia
- 1 teaspoon vanilla extract

Directions:

1. Take a bowl and mix eggs, stevia, and vanilla extract.
2. Pour this mixture in the blender and blend until smooth.
3. Put the butter and chocolate in the pot of Ninja Foodi and press sauté.
4. Sauté for 2 minutes until the chocolate is melted.
5. Add the melted chocolate into the egg mixture.
6. Pour the mixture in the baking mold and place it in the Ninja Foodi.
7. Press "Bake/Roast" and set the timer for about 30 minutes at 360 degrees F.
8. Bake for about 30 minutes, cut into pieces and serve.

Nutrition:

- Calories 266

- Total Fat 26.9 g
- Saturated Fat 15.8 g
- Cholesterol 184 mg
- Sodium 218 mg
- Total Carbs 2.5 g
- Fiber 0 g
- Sugar 0.4 g
- Protein 4.5 g

10.15 Cream Crepes

Prep Time: 15 minutes

Cooking time: 16 minutes

Servings: 6

Ingredients:
- 1½ teaspoons Splenda
- 3 organic eggs
- 3 tablespoons coconut flour
- ½ cup heavy cream
- 3 tablespoons coconut oil, melted and divided
- Salt to taste

Directions:
1. Take a bowl and mix 1½ tablespoons of coconut oil, Splenda, eggs, and salt.
2. Add the coconut flour and continuously stir.
3. Add the heavy cream and stir continuously until smooth.

4. Press sauté on Ninja Foodi and pour about ¼ of the mixture in the pot.
5. Sauté for 2 minutes on each side and dish out.
6. Repeat until the mixture ends and serve.

Nutrition:
- Calories 145
- Total Fat 13.1 g
- Saturated Fat 9.1 g
- Cholesterol 96 mg,
- Sodium 35 mg
- Total Carbs 4 g
- Fiber 1.5 g
- Sugar 1.2 g
- Protein 3.5 g

10.16 Nut Porridge

Prep Time: 15 minutes
Cooking time: 10 minutes
Servings: 4
Ingredients:
- 4 teaspoons coconut oil, melted
- 1 cup pecans, halved
- 2 cups of water
- 2 tablespoons stevia
- 1 cup cashew nuts, raw and unsalted

Directions:

1. Put the cashew nuts and pecans in the precision processor and pulse till they are in chunks.
2. Put this mixture into the pot of Ninja Foodi and stir in water, coconut oil and stevia.
3. Select sauté on Ninja Foodi and cook for 15 minutes.
4. Serve and enjoy.

Nutrition:

- Calories 260,
- Total Fat 22.9 g,
- Saturated Fat 7.3 g,
- Cholesterol 0 mg,
- Sodium 9 mg,
- Total Carbs 12.7 g,
- Fiber 1.4 g,
- Sugar 1.8 g,
- Protein 5.6 g

11. Conclusion

This cookbook tried to offer you a large array of recipes using a new cooking appliance; the revolutionary Ninja Foodi, which combines pressure cookers, Air Fryers, Ovens and Dehydrator at the same time. And if you haven't heard about the Ninja Foodi, you should start reading this book, because not only will it offer some of the most sumptuous recipes that you can ever stumble into, but it will also offer you useful information that will help you understand the function of this new cooking appliance. So, if you are a Newbie in the use of Ninja Foodies, don't get frustrated, because in this book, you will just find everything you need and enough information that will help you understand this cooking appliance better.

So, if you have made your purchase of Ninja Foodi lately; you shouldn't be afraid, because with the help of this book; you will be able to master the use of this revolutionary cooking appliance. Besides; this book will offer you some of the most important tips that may help you using Ninja Foodies perfectly from the first use.

Thereby, with the introduction of Ninja Pressure cookers to your Kitchen and world; you can discover yourself a culinary revolution that has affected the various Kitchen gadgets with the unique cooking appliance, Ninja Pressure Cookers. Ninja Foodi has, indeed, been considered as a more impressive kitchen appliance that many conventional cooking gadgets and appliances. And all the people who have tried using Ninja Foodies find it more impressive and very easy to use. And what most of the people like about the Ninja Foodi is that it can act as an air Fryer, a pressure cooker, a roaster, a slow cooker, a steamer, a dehydrator and more.

So, if you are looking for a unique cooking appliance that can save your money as you will give up on purchasing many cooking appliances at once; this cookbook is the perfect choice for you. And in this book; you will find 100 recipes that vary from breakfast recipes to snacks, appetizers, poultry and different types of meats as well as desserts and vegetable food.

And what makes this book more special is that you will be able to turn out any type of ingredients into the dish you want in a very short time and you will still get the same delicious taste you are looking for with the simplest ingredients. And whether you want a crispy recipe; a tender one; a roasted taste; you will be able to get it all.

And if you have any doubts about this cooking appliance because it is new and you don't have so much information about it; all you have to do is to download your copy of this book right away because it will clear out any types of ambiguity you have. Get ready to read this book because it will offer you a mixture of everything you need to learn about Ninja Foodies, its benefits, use and more.

So, if you have made your purchase of Ninja Foodi lately; you shouldn't be afraid, because with the help of this book; you will be able to master the use of this revolutionary cooking appliance. Besides; this book will offer you some of the most important tips that may help you using Ninja Foodies perfectly from the first use.

www.ingramcontent.com/pod-product-compliance
Lightning Source LLC
Chambersburg PA
CBHW081400070526
44583CB00020B/2611